Lama Surya Das has spent over thirty years studying with the great spiritual masters of Asia, including the Dalai Lama, and is a leading spokesperson for the emerging American Buddhism and contemporary spirituality. He is an authorized Lama in the Dzogchen lineage of Tibet. A poet, translator, and full-time spiritual teacher, he leads lectures, workshops, and meditation retreats worldwide. He is the author of three books, including the national bestseller *Awakening the Buddha Within*, is active in interfaith dialogue, and has been featured in numerous publications including *New Age Journal*, the *Boston Globe*, the *Los Angeles Times*, and *Tricycle*. He lives in Concord, Massachusetts.

AWAKENING THE BUDDHIST HEART
Lama Surya Das

'Surya Das's book brings to life the timeless wisdom of Buddhism in traditional teaching stories and heartfelt everyday examples. Anyone on a spiritual path will recognize themselves in these pages and find both inspiration and practical advice'
Sharon Salzburg, author of *A Heart as Wide as the World*

'This brilliant, amusing, and wise book is the perfect distillation of ancient spiritual wisdom for our times. Practical and down-to-earth, written by one of the greatest American dharma teachers, it has the power to awaken you to an ever-deepening relationship with all of life. What a precious jewel you hold in your hand. Use it with joy'
**Joan Borysenko, Ph.D., author of
*Minding the Body, Me..***

'*Awakening the Buddhist Heart* cont: as any book I know. It will help y becoming more wise, more compa
Sam Keen, author of

www.booksattransworld.co.uk

Cultivating Love

and Spiritual

Intelligence

in Your Life

BANTAM BOOKS

LONDON · NEW YORK · TORONTO · SYDNEY · AUCKLAND

AWAKENING
THE
BUDDHIST
HEART

Lama Surya Das

AWAKENING THE BUDDHIST HEART
A BANTAM BOOK : 0 553 81366 8

First publication in Great Britain

PRINTING HISTORY
Bantam Press edition published 2001

1 3 5 7 9 10 8 6 4 2

Set in Bembo by
Phoenix Typesetting, Ilkley, West Yorkshire.

Bantam Books are published by Transworld Publishers,
61–63 Uxbridge Road, London W5 5SA,
a division of The Random House Group Ltd,
in Australia by Random House Australia (Pty) Ltd,
20 Alfred Street, Milsons Point, Sydney, NSW 2061, Australia,
in New Zealand by Random House New Zealand Ltd,
18 Poland Road, Glenfield, Auckland 10, New Zealand
and in South Africa by Random House (Pty) Ltd,
Endulini, 5a Jubilee Road, Parktown 2193, South Africa.

Printed and bound in Great Britain by
Clays Ltd, St Ives plc.

To my late Dzogchen master,

Nyoshul Khenpo Rinpoche

1932–1999

ACKNOWLEDGMENTS

I want to gratefully acknowledge the good friends whose encouragement and assistance helped make this book possible, and who all help me to open my very own heart.

Thank you to Lauren Marino, my fine editor at Broadway Books; Susan Lee Cohen, my literary agent; Julie Coopersmith, who always reminds me to go deeper and helps make it all possible; and Kathy Peterson, for her loving support and 'being there'.

I also want to thank my copy editor Nancy Peske, my assistant Julie Barker, as well as all the friends and colleagues who shared their many stories and gave support and encouragement, especially Maggie Sluyter, Deb Bouvier, Ram Dass, John Halley, Lucy Duggan, Christopher Coriat, Chad Gillette, Paul Crafts, Ron Goldman, Charles Genoud, John Makransky, Roger Walsh, Michele Tempesta, Vincent Duggan, Philip Carter, and Cheryl Pelavin.

Contents

CONTENTS

Nothing worth doing is completed
In one lifetime,
Therefore we must be saved by hope.
Nothing true or beautiful makes
Complete sense
In any context of history,
Therefore we must be saved by faith.
Nothing we do, no matter how virtuous,
Can be accomplished alone.
Therefore we must be saved by love.

– Reinhold Niebuhr

INTRODUCTION

The Buddhist heart is alive and well in all of us. It is just a matter of awakening to it. This luminous spiritual jewel is what the Dalai Lama calls 'the good heart,' representing our own inner goodness – our most tender, compassionate, and caring side. That is why the Dalai Lama always says, 'My religion is loving-kindness.' The loving heart is our share of the true, good, and beautiful – something genuine to cherish and venerate.

This basic goodness is our true nature, or Buddha-nature – our highest, wisest self. Our best Self. It is like the little Buddha within each of us. This radiant innate jewel represents what we aspire toward as well as who we truly *are*. These two aspects – a developmental, growth-oriented, 'higher educational' side and the innate, timeless, immanent side – are like two sides of a single hand. It is a helping hand as well as a hand that is complete in itself. This is what Tibet's Dzogchen masters call 'Buddhahood in the palm of your hand'; it is all right there. You may feel far from it, but it is never far from you.

As we enter a new century and a new millennium, and in the light of all the challenges, changes, and uncertainty we must face daily, it seems increasingly important to awaken our Buddha-like hearts through spiritual connections. We can make spiritual connections within ourselves, with all the various aspects and facets of ourselves and our life – physical, mental, emotional, psychological, spiritual – recognizing that everything we do and feel is part of our spiritual journey.

What better time to awaken our hearts and make meaningful connections with others as well through the avenue of friendship and relationship? We can do this with our families, our romantic partners, and our colleagues, through work, with our neighbors, our society, our country, and our world; we can do this with our pets and animals and all creatures, great and small. Moreover we can extend ourselves to include in our radiant heart's awakened embrace all things, animate and inanimate – everything that is in our natural environment. And we can connect with that which is greater than, yet within and all around, each of us.

Where better to make this spiritual connection than here and now, with our best selves and with each other, in every part of our lives? Awakening the Buddhist heart that beats within each of us will bring us directly into intimate relatedness to one and to all, unveiling our innate spiritual connectedness to the source and ground of our very being, thus informing every aspect of our daily lives with purpose, meaning, and love.

CHAPTER ONE

*Spiritual Intelligence —
Connecting to the Bigger Picture*

Life is about relationship – the relationship we have with ourselves, with each other, with the world, as well as the connection to that which is beyond any of us yet immanent in each of us. When our relationships are good, we feel good; when they are bad, we feel awful. Let's accept it. We need each other. We need to feel connected; we need to feel each other's presence and love.

The most ancient scriptures of India say that we are all part of a universal web of light. Each of us is a glowing, shining, mirrorlike jewel reflecting and containing the light of the whole. All in one. One in all. We are never disconnected from the whole. This intrinsic knowledge of our place in the greater picture is part of our spiritual DNA, our original software – or 'heartware.'

Nonetheless, at one time or another most of us feel disconnected from this knowledge of our place in the great web of being. We lose sight of where we

17

belong, and instead, we experience intense feelings of loneliness, alienation, and confusion. Trying to find the way back to our place in the whole is what the spiritual seeker's search is all about. It represents a journey home to who we are.

How about you? Do you ever suffer from a sense that you are lost and wandering – almost as though you have been through some kind of an emotional holocaust? Most of us here in America are very fortunate. We have little idea of what it's like to live in a war-torn country. Even so, from the safety of your own secure home, do you sometimes feel as though you have an uncanny sense of what it must feel like to be a displaced person – unsafe and at the mercy of strangers? Mother Teresa said, 'The biggest problem facing the world today is not people dying in the streets of Calcutta, and not inflation, but spiritual deprivation . . . this feeling of emptiness associated with feeling separate from God, and from all our sisters and brothers on planet earth.' 'Loneliness,' she said, 'is like the leprosy of the West.'

Mother Teresa was talking about the pain associated with feelings of isolation and separateness. These feelings are common to mankind. They can overtake any one of us in a heartbeat, even in the very midst of happiness and joy. Loneliness implies a lack of meaningful connection. For most people, it is a familiar travelling companion. Even when we're surrounded by people we know, we can feel separate and apart. Separate from what, we might ask? Separate from others, separate from ourselves, separate from the Divine, separate from meaning, separate from love. Separate from a sense of belonging.

The promise of spiritual life is that we will be able to heal these feelings through love and an experiential understanding of the essential interconnectedness of all beings. The Dalai Lama of Tibet, for example, often says that no matter how many new faces he sees each day, he never feels as though he is meeting anyone for the first time. That's because the Dalai Lama knows that every single one of us is on an infinite journey that began aeons ago. According to Tibetan Buddhism we have each had so many births that in all probability our paths have crossed time and time again. Wondrously connected one to the other, we have been for each other brothers, sisters, cousins, aunts, children, fathers, mothers, and mates. At the heart of Tibetan Buddhism is this belief: Each person we meet has at one time been a close, caring family member and should be treated with the respect and love such a relationship deserves.

Don't we all need to feel the light and warmth that emanates from others? Don't we all want true love? Don't we all hunger for genuine communication, and deeper and more authentic connections? Don't we all recognize that the quality of our individual lives is determined by the quality of our relationships both external and internal? When our relationships are superficial, we feel as though we are leading superficial lives; when our relationships reflect our deeper commitments and aspirations, we feel as though we are walking a more meaningful and satisfying path.

Love comes through relating. That's why we must connect.

Connecting to the sacred in our relationships is a way of satisfying our spiritual hunger with love – thus nurturing ourselves, as well as nourishing the world. For just a minute, stop and think about your relationships. Think about all those with whom you interact – at home, at work, and in the community. Think about family, friends, coworkers, and even those with whom you have only a nodding acquaintance. Don't leave anybody out, not even your pets. Whenever you think about the important relationships in your life, remember that each of us also has a connection with the natural world and all the wild creatures that live on our planet – as well as with the planet itself.

Some of our relationships seem deep and meaningful; others are merely casual. But on a spiritual level, they are all important; they can all be deepened and improved. Relationships are essential for ongoing spiritual growth and development. They help us find meaning and purpose; they help us experience love – human as well as divine. Learning to love is the first lesson in Spirituality 101. The connections we make as we live our incredible lives offer us the opportunity to acknowledge and connect to the divine in ourselves as well as in others. Ask yourself: Who did you love today?

Although spiritual seekers and saints historically have often been associated with self-sacrifice and reclusive, solitary lifestyles (often monastic, and frequently cloistered), here in the modern world, other traditions and styles of spirituality are emerging. Contemporary seekers realize that we can't retreat permanently; it is not very helpful to pass negative judgments on worldly values. Instead we need to find new and better ways of walking the soulful path of awakening, by integrating the heart of love in every aspect of our lives.

In this way we learn to dance gracefully with life.

It is a fundamental Buddhist tenet as well as a larger, more general fact of life that we are all interconnected and inter-dependent on each other. I find it very gratifying to see that so many Western seekers and students of truth and Dharma are sincerely striving to combine social activism with spiritual growth. As seekers, we want to find ways to do spiritual work within our relationships. We aspire to help improve the quality of our own lives as well as the lives of those around us. In this way we are hopeful that we will be better able to live in congruence with our most deeply held inner principles and values. We who inhabit this planet all share a common karma as well as a common ground. We already live together; we need to learn to work together. We need to learn to love others — even those we may not like. This is the greatest challenge of all.

For the sake of clarity, Tibetan teachings traditionally divide our spiritual efforts and practices into two categories:

✳ Inner — those efforts we make primarily for ourselves

✳ Outer — those efforts we make primarily for the benefit of others and the world around us

The inner-directed goal of a spiritual life is to realize the innate purity and primordial perfection in each of us. This expresses itself in how we see — and treat — ourselves. Through inner work, we realize the truth, wisdom, clarity, and peace of mind that is latent in each of us. No one else can give it to us or provide it for us. We must find it for ourselves.

The outer goal expresses itself in how we feel about others, how we perceive them, as well as how we treat them. By learning to better love and care for ourselves as well as each other, we get closer to that which is greater than any one of us. When we serve and foster one soul, we serve the whole world. This is spiritual connection. Through spiritual practice, we connect in all directions at once – a little like tuning into some vast cosmic Internet. As we refine our outer and inner efforts, becoming more and more skillful through practice, we realize that these efforts are one. The great naturalist John Muir once said, 'I only went out for a walk and finally concluded to stay out till sundown, for going out, I found, was really going in.'

What does this mean for us day to day as we go about our lives at home, in the office, or at the shopping mall? As seekers, we want to be able to improve our relationships at work; we want personal connections that bring us the abundance and joy they initially promise. How can we grow together spiritually with the people we care about? How can we share meditation, silence, song, and prayer with those we love? How can we spiritually enrich every relationship?

We all have special bonds with certain people, including those we may even think of as 'soul mates.' But what about the bonds we share with people we don't love or respect? What about people toward whom we feel anger, annoyance, distrust, and contempt? What can we learn from those we love as well as those we don't? Can we, for example, learn to love people we don't even like? Buddhist teachings tell us that all of our bonds are sacred; they remind us that sometimes our adversaries provide us with the most precious teachings. We never really do anything alone; we always have help, even though sometimes that help comes in very strange forms. We are surrounded by an array of helping, loving hands.

One of the most difficult things we all struggle with are feelings of existential despair – a sense that there is little or no meaning or purpose to our existence. Sometimes it just all seems too much, and we lose our sense of place, our feeling of fitting in, of being understood, of belonging. As much as we may be rushing here and there, we don't always know where we are going. We haven't found our bearings, the polestar of our existence. We just keep on keepin' on with no respite in sight.

Spiritual teachings universally remind us that we are integral and essential parts of a greater pattern. There is an exquisite meaning and coherence to life. I'm not talking now about a perfectly ordered theistic universe or a fixed destiny. What I'm describing are cosmic principles and universal laws that are always at work. I believe we can discover and align ourselves with these principles, perhaps even become masters of them. No matter how lost we may be, it is possible to find our place within the whole. We *can* get 'there' from here – wherever here may be for you right now. 'Here,' after all, is within the word 'there.'

Life sometimes seems so chaotic, like a terrifying maelstrom that exists only to whip us about. But in truth, it's really more like a mandala or hologram. There are constellations, patterns, and even directions to be found within the vastness and mystery of it all. At the end of my freshman year of college, I came back to stay with my parents on Long Island, and I took a summer job at a law firm in Manhattan. I remember what it felt like on my commute to work each morning, popping out of a subterranean, dark, Bosch-like netherworld of subways and train tunnels, not knowing exactly where I was. During my first days at my job, I walked out onto the teeming streets during lunch hour, and all I knew was that I was some-place in midtown, whatever *that* meant. People were swirling around like floodwaters in those concrete canyons amidst skyscrapers that were so densely constructed that even at midday, the sun was completely hidden. I had no orientation, no sense of direction. Where was I? I remember walking around with no idea of where I was going, feeling somewhat nervous that I would not find my way back to the office, and then suddenly I came upon a bus stop and a blow-up map of Manhattan. I saw that if I wanted to amble, it was just a short walk to Central Park and an easy stroll to the Museum of Modern Art. Rockefeller Center was just a block or two away, and if I wanted to venture further after work, I could get on the Fifth Avenue bus and go straight down to Greenwich Village, a favorite teenage haunt of mine. The large blow-up subway map provided me with a view from above, instantly rescuing me from the bewildered feeling that I was lost in a maze. I knew where I was, and I knew what was around me, and I saw how it all fit together.

Spiritually speaking, we've all experienced feelings of being so lost in the dense thickets of our lives that we can't see the paths or figure out how large the forest really is. At those times we lack an overview, a world map, an awareness of the bigger picture. But some people seem to have a deeper and better sense of who they are, where they are standing, and where they are going. They seem to have a better sense of how to navigate the highways and byways of life without losing their way. Simply put, they seem to have a better sense of their spiritual center. This is like having an internal compass, an internal true-ing device.

FINDING A SPIRITUAL CENTER

Just as the unexamined life is a life poorly lived, no life is complete without some effort to connect with the deeper meaning of our existence. Whether we are Jewish, Christian, Buddhist, Hindu, Muslim, or non-believer, we all have spiritual DNA; that graceful, radiant inner spiral connects us above and below, leading both within and without.

When we, as seekers, begin to reconnect more deeply with our loving hearts – our spiritual centers – we begin to achieve greater realization of the profound wisdom and intuitive awareness that is a natural part of each of us. This is spiritual intelligence; it naturally recognizes the heart connection and the inseparability of self and other.

When we take standard IQ tests, what we're being tested for is our ability to see the connections between things – numbers, words, mathematical concepts, and geometric shapes. Spiritual intelligence is very similar. People whose spiritual intelligence is highly developed are able to see the connecting patterns and principles that help create meaning and order out of the seeming chaos of life. Spiritual intelligence gives us the wisdom to see the relationship between the whole and its many parts, the one and the many, the ordinary and the extraordinary, the mundane and the divine, the light and its shadow. Spiritual intelligence is existential awareness.

The more we cultivate our innate spiritual intelligence, the more we become aware of and intuitively sensitive to what those around us see and feel. Cultivating a heightened spiritual discernment and awareness helps us become better mates, parents, and friends. Ultimately it can lead us to mind reading, clairvoyance, healing powers, shape shifting, and the development of other psychic abilities as well as deepening our inner wisdom and compassion.

Over the years, a fair amount of esoteric material has been written about Tibet – some fascinating, some strange at best. Many Westerners, for example, including a number of my friends and contemporaries, initially became interested in learning more about Tibet through the eccentric writings of a man who called himself Lobsang Rampa. Rampa, who was in fact a British plumber, presented himself to readers as a Tibetan lama. Later, when it was discovered that this was an Englishman who had never even been to Tibet, Rampa announced that a Tibetan lama had taken hold of his body, and that he, Rampa, was channeling this information.

Rampa's most famous book, which was a bestseller in the U.S. and England some forty years ago, was called *The Third Eye*. In it, there is a very dramatic scene that takes place in the bowels of the Potala Palace, the centuries-old home of a succession of Dalai Lamas, all of whom were during their life-times the spiritual and political leaders of Tibet. In this fictional scene, the then Dalai Lama goes down to the deep basement which holds the gold-plated, lotus-positioned, mummified remains of previous Dalai Lamas. There, he subjects himself to an operation in which a wooden corkscrew is used to open his 'third eye,' the inner wisdom eye located in the center of the forehead.

I've been to the Potala Palace, and I've seen the gilded embalmed remains in their tomb monuments. But the corkscrew operation should not be taken literally. It's obviously a fictional technology. However, the concept of an inner wisdom eye, an eye that is so spiritually aware that it sees beyond everyday illusion, is not so farfetched. In fact, one of the first books by the present Dalai Lama is called *Opening the Wisdom Eye*.

For Tibetans, the possibility of heightened awareness is taken for granted; in fact it is often raised to the level of science and is even part of medical procedure. New York City's master Buddhist professor, Robert Thurman, describing Tibetan medical diagnosis, writes:

'The trained Tibetan doctor develops a combination of memorization, anatomical learning, subtle visualization and contemplative heightening of sensitivity. He or she trains the six tip corners of the first three fingers of each hand to be attuned to the twelve channels of communication from the patient's body. Placing these fingers anywhere on the body . . . but preferably on the radial arteries of the two wrists, the doctor becomes a psychic CAT-scan machine. He or she lets the awareness enter into the body of the patient, travel through the blood, lymph and neural systems into various organs and vessels, and emerge with a detailed picture of the exact physical condition of the patient's body.'

We all can learn to raise our spiritual intelligence and heighten the power of our incandescent awareness. If we elevate our gaze and open wide our wisdom eyes, ears, and innermost tender hearts, our spiritual intelligence will soar. We will possess higher knowledge as well as uncommon common sense. This is the sacred intelligence that can help create win/win scenarios in all our relationships.

THE COMPONENTS OF
SPIRITUAL INTELLIGENCE

What is spiritual intelligence? And how do we get it? How can we each find a higher or deeper transcendent spiritual vision and perspective? Some vegetarians say that it's spiritual to be vegetarian; people who are kosher believe that it's spiritually necessary to be kosher. In Judaism, following the Torah is spiritually intelligent. The word 'Islam' means surrender or submission to God's will; in Islam, surrendering to God's will is spiritual intelligence. That's not so different from Taoism where spiritual intelligence is equated with learning to be one with the flow of things, the Tao. Some people might say we become more spiritually intelligent by meditating and sitting around trying not to think. However, Tibetan lamas say that when we practice that type of mind-wiping meditation we run the risk of being reborn as cows – dumbly chewing their cud over and over again.

But all of this seems very generalized and is missing a certain specificity. From where I sit, spiritual intelligence has three separate components. They are:

1. A SENSE OF THE BIGGER PICTURE

Have you ever tried to look at the world with a God's eye view – an overarching or divine point of view? Think about this for a minute. Even if you don't believe in God – and most Buddhists don't – imagine what an omniscient being would see. Some say that Buddha, who was perfectly enlightened, was omniscient. What do you think he perceived as he lived an enlightened life? Remember that the Buddha himself said he was able to remember at least five hundred previous lifetimes. From his unique vantage point, it would be almost impossible to become overly invested in petty day-to-day problems. I think the Buddha, who often referred to his students and followers as children, had seen so many things come and go that he was able to keep everything in perspective.

I spend a lot of time flying around the country on teaching tours, and I love looking out of the plane window while passing over places like the Rocky Mountains, the Great Lakes, the midwestern farmlands and plains, great rivers like the Mississippi, and large man-made cities too. When you fly over the Grand Canyon, the pilot often points it out, and everyone looks out the window. I like peering down over rows of neatly laid out houses on streets that from a distance look like accessories for a miniature model train layout. From thousands of feet up in the air, even New York City appears to be a gleaming anthill. I love being high above the clouds where the sun is always shining. This reminds me of deep spiritual memories, of a sacred timeless time and spacious space. The feeling is one of *been there, known that*.

From the perspective of being high up in a plane, we get a small sense of the bigger picture, the long view, the eagle's vision. Most spiritual traditions make a special place for elders, those members of the community whose age and experience makes it easier for them to offer a larger, wiser perspective on life. As we mature spiritually and become elder-like in our attitude toward life, it becomes easier to get beyond our own petty prejudices and short-term thinking and move further away from selfishness and self-interest toward stewardship and guardianship.

When we take the long view, we are better able to be spiritually intelligent in our relationships. Margot, for example, is very upset that her son, Josh, failed a geometry test. She's worried about Josh getting into a good college, and because of this she's been coming down pretty hard on him. When she is able to step back and take a God's eye view, she can see that it's just a small test, and not the major calamity that she fears. Life will go on . . . and on. Still, it is hard to remember that sometimes.

My friend Patti says that when her son was three and a half

years old, he had a table with four little chairs, and he used to lug one of the chairs with him everywhere, climbing on it and turning it upside down. He was really rough on those chairs. First one broke, then another, and finally a third. Patti got angry at the little boy. 'Can't you be more careful?' she said in an angry tone of voice. Her son started crying. 'Mommy,' he said, his little lip trembling, 'I'm your only son, and you're making me feel bad because of a chair.' Patti said that even though her son is still a little kid, he exhibited a wisdom that was, at that moment, superior to her own.

If we're going to relate to others successfully, we need a firm sense of perspective and a clear idea about what's important in the long run. That means that often we have to let go of our rigid ideas and fixed positions on a wide variety of things. We need to focus on those values and virtues that we know are important in the long run and let go of some of the issues and concerns that are fundamentally superficial or even comic. Sometimes when we look at life with a long view, all we can do is laugh at our foibles. Doesn't it sometimes seem as though we are all Moe, Larry, and Curly, continuously falling all over ourselves in our clumsy silliness?

Buddhism teaches that we are usually feeling something – pleasure, displeasure, or indifference. But these feelings change, all the time. We have good years, and we have bad years; good hair days and bad hair days. We can be elated one week, sad the next. We can be calm one moment, excited the next. Nothing stays the same. The long view helps us let go of our attachment to feelings that aren't giving us real satisfaction.

2. THE ABILITY TO DISTINGUISH THE REAL FROM THE UNREAL

It is taught that when the Buddha achieved perfect enlightenment, the veil of illusion was lifted from in front of his eyes. He was able to see truth; he was able to perceive reality. Illusion and delusion are part of the human condition. In a world that is filled with deceit, manipulation, and exploitation, not to mention spin doctors, it's easy to get cynical about truth. It's easy to become confused about what we're really hearing, seeing, experiencing, or feeling; it's too easy to believe what we're told, even when, in our heart of hearts, we know it's not true.

The Buddha saw and experienced life with perfect clarity of vision. Keep in mind that when the Buddha began his path, he was a human being, like you and me. When the Buddha became enlightened, he still retained all his humanity, but he had transcended his human limitations and attachment to mere appearances. He realized freedom and deathless bliss, 'nirvana.'

The Buddha became enlightened through his own efforts. If he were living today, indeed if he were one of our neighbors, we might look at him and say, 'Wow, that guy really keeps working on himself.' The Buddha's hard work paid off; through his efforts, he was able to realize absolute truth – ultimate reality. In Buddhism, the true nature of the world is called 'sunyata,' or emptiness/openness.

Most of us, of course, have to be content with relative truth or relative reality. Because we believe in the possibility of enlightenment, however, we continue to strive toward the deepest truth. The path to ultimate reality takes hard work. If we value truth and reality, we do this work by chipping away at the falsehoods, both large and subtle, in our own lives. If we continue to look at any object or situation and use our minds to peel away the layers of projections, concepts, and reactivity, we get closer and closer to reality and absolute truth – things just as they are, in all their naked, unalloyed splendor. That's part of becoming more and more enlightened. We can become a little more illumined every day that we walk the path.

Take a book off a shelf and look at it. At first glance it looks like paper and print, but get beyond mere surface appearances, and think about the ink and the trees that created the paper. If you were to try to get that book down to its most basic form, you would have to consider atomic and molecular structure. And what about the words in the book you're examining? Do they reflect truth? Does the book convey different levels of meaning? Many of us have had the experience of reading and rereading a book, finding new and deeper truths each time.

The search for truth is the seeker's search. We keep analyzing, reflecting on, and unwrapping the experiences we encounter in an attempt to find fundamental truth. Every day we can bring the search for truth to our dealings with friends, family, and coworkers. All we need to do is make truth a value, a touchstone. All things flow from that commitment.

Recently I was in a shoe store with a woman friend who was trying to buy some sandals. As I sat there waiting, somewhat impatiently, I noticed an elderly woman who was trying to find a pair of sneakers that fit. 'None of them are right,' she complained. 'They're either too big or too small. In this one, my big toe is hitting against the end of the shoe.' She was with several family members who were trying to convince her that the sneakers she had on *did* indeed fit, and that she was imagining the tightness, and she was wavering in her conviction. Finally, just as her family and the salesperson had finished convincing her that she should buy the pair she had on, another woman, a senior citizen with beautifully dyed red hair, entered the store and sat down next to her. 'Tell me,' the first woman said to the newcomer. 'Do you think this sneaker is too tight?' 'Let me see,' said the redhead. She reached down and poked the sneaker with her thumb. 'Absolutely,' she decreed. 'Your big toe is hitting the side. You're not going to be able to walk in them.' I could see the first woman's entire family groan silently and roll their eyes up in unison.

This little vignette was a classic lesson in reality. If the woman had brought home the sneakers, and they pinched her big toe, she would have had to live with the consequences. This kind of thing happens to all of us. We fail to acknowledge the truth of what's happening in our own lives as it's taking place. We see what we want to see, hear what we want to hear, and ignore the messages we find distasteful. As a result we end up living our lives feeling the pinch. We ignore reality every time we spend money we don't have; we ignore reality every time we close our eyes to our own unhappiness or the suffering of those around us; and we ignore reality every time we construct fantasies that help us avoid what we don't want to see.

The Buddha saw 'what is.' He saw things exactly as they are. This may sound ordinary, but in fact, it's totally extra-ordinary. You may think that everybody sees reality, but check it out. I'm sure you'll discover that we can all walk down the same street, and yet we'll see and hear different things. One person's flower is another person's pollen season. A firm grip on reality helps us be aware of both the flower and the pollen.

3. AN UNDERSTANDING OF KARMA – CAUSE AND EFFECT

Your karma is the result of everything you do, think, say, and feel. Right now, it's a summer day, and this morning the room in which I am working is hotter than normal. Yesterday I failed to pull the blinds on the west side of the house, and the blazing afternoon sun heated my study all day long. Now I'm uncomfortable. I'm also at least partially responsible. That's karma. There is no one else to blame.

The thing about karma is that everything we do has some consequence. For every cause there is an effect. Buddhism teaches that our karma was created by past behavior – some of it in other lifetimes, some of it within the last hour. It also teaches that no matter when karma is created, it can be changed, worked with, expiated, purified, and transformed. That means our destiny is in our own hands.

Understanding karma helps us get more accurate insight into how things work. The teachings about karma explain causation and show us how things fit together. The Buddha taught that all psychological and physical phenomena are interdependent. He said that everything we do, say, or even think conditions the next act, word, or thought. This, one of the most essential Buddhist teachings, is known as the Chain of Conditioned Arising.

Let's say, for example, that when you were a child, your mother hated being in the city in the summer and took you to the country, and you enjoyed the experience. You responded to her negative feelings about the city, and you also liked the experience of being in the country. Now as an adult, when you are forced to spend your summer weekends in a city, you feel acutely deprived; you respond more positively to the smells, sights, and sounds of the country. One day, you go to visit a friend who lives in a bucolic area; strolling through town, you see some local real estate ads. Impulsively you walk into a real estate agency, and before the day ends you make an offer for a small house and sign a large check.

Now, how does this work? You have an impulse based on past experiences. Your impulse leads to a thought; the thought becomes a movement (words and deeds) that will bring you to the country each weekend. This establishes a pattern. Through repetition, a pattern becomes a habit. You may now regularly find yourself on a crowded highway driving to and from the country every weekend during rush hour. Habitual patterns help form our character, which in turn determine our destiny. This is karmic evolution. This is how we constantly shape and reshape our lives – for better or for worse.

Each impulse we have lays down an imprint; when it's repeated it becomes a groove. The groove creates a channel, and energy as well as more material things start to be pulled and channeled more and more in that direction. Once a groove is firmly established, it's hard to change. If we want to alter our behavior, we have to make strong conscious efforts to do so. Buddhist teachings about karma tell us that every time we do something, we are psychologically, physically, emotionally, and even morally imprinted and conditioned in a way that makes it more likely that we will behave the same way the next time.

When we want to change the way we are with ourselves or with the rest of the world, we need to do a little karmic intervention in order to alter old habits and behavior patterns. This is very difficult. Joanna, for example, approaches most situations passively. She has never been able to take a proactive approach, and she has suffered accordingly. Right now, she is struggling to become more direct, assertive, and outspoken in her life. For her, this is very hard work. I know other people who find Joanna's passive approach to life unfathomable. Joanna's friend Sarah treats every situation as though it is a potential battle zone; she is always trying to restrain her tendencies to jump in and take over. Both Joanna and Sarah realize that changing their behavior will change their experiences and their destiny. When we change our attitudes as well as our intentions, wishes, and aspirations, we are able to change our behavior and thus change our karma. This is the first principle of self-mastery and the Buddhist practices that bring inner freedom and autonomy.

One of the most important teachings about karma is this: It's not what happens to us that matters most; it's what we do with it. Yesterday a student who was about to go on retreat called me. She told me that one of her tires went flat while she was driving in the country during a rainstorm. She had never bothered to sign up for any road service like AAA; she had a cell phone, but the battery was dead; she was wearing shorts and a T-shirt and had no umbrella or warm clothing in the car. She used her flat tire as a learning experience. As soon as she got home, she became a member of a road service; she purchased a device so she could charge her phone from the car battery; she put an umbrella, a heavy sweatshirt, and a blanket in the trunk of her car; and she got some flares and a flashlight as well. To learn from experience makes us grow wiser with our years.

I often meet people who say to me, 'Everything in my life is a mess, so I guess I must have done something wrong in my past life. . . . Haha!' I find this approach to problems somewhat distressing. The Buddha said, 'If you want to know what your future life will be like, look at your life right now.' We are creating the future, and we are doing it today. We always have choices. We all have to fight the impulse to become rigid caricatures of the people and personality types we have always been. It is spiritually intelligent to stay open to new possibilities and new ways of being. Just because we – or our parents or grandparents – have always acted in a certain way doesn't mean it has to continue. We are not victims of our past; we all have choices. If a behavior or way of thinking doesn't have the positive payoff of making our lives happy, it can and should be changed. We could all afford to be a little more flexible and adaptable. Understanding the law of karma helps us do that.

Seekers living today have tremendous spiritual mobility, not just to change their religions, but to change their karmic behavior patterns. Change is now a positive value in our society, and we have many more tools at our disposal than earlier generations had. We don't have to travel great distances to find the best teachers to help us. We can read their books, watch videotapes, or listen to audiotapes; we can connect with many of them on their websites or on-line. We can go into therapy in order to change patterns that no longer work. We can attend seminars and support groups. We can talk openly to friends in a way that earlier generations would not have dreamed possible. These opportunities are part of our collective karma; spiritual intelligence reminds us to take advantage of them.

CONNECTING TO THE BIGGER PICTURE – A PRACTICE

Kalu Rinpoche, who died in 1989 at his monastery in Darjeeling, India, was one of the great Tibetan meditation masters of his time. When I first went to India, I lived there in his monastery off and on for eight years. One of the first teachings Kalu Rinpoche gave was known as the Four Mind Changers. It's an ancient practice designed to help us connect to a deeper reality.

This reflective exercise is a basic Buddhist preliminary practice. This kind of examination helps us turn our hearts and minds to Dharma – truth and reality – and away from worldliness, confusion, and ordinary habits; it sharpens our spiritual intelligence by raising our consciousness and heightening our awareness about who we are and how we all fit together in this world and this universe. Kalu Rinpoche advised that we practice it before we begin any meditation or prayer session, but this kind of reflection can be done at any time – while taking a walk, riding a subway, or waiting for a bus.

This reflection on four basic thoughts can help us sort out our values and priorities and become more conscientious about our spiritual practice. We use this exercise to keep us grounded in reality and conscious of what's truly important.

Reflect on the following:

I

I HAVE BEEN BLESSED WITH A LIFE IN WHICH I CAN DO MANY THINGS TO FURTHER MY OWN HAPPINESS AND THE HAPPINESS OF THOSE AROUND ME.

Life is an amazing opportunity filled with freedoms and choices too wondrous to describe. It would be a shame to waste this wondrous opportunity by engaging in useless and meaningless activities; it would be a pity to waste this life by not fulfilling one's spiritual potential. The chances that exist for each of us today to be more loving, kind, helpful, and compassionate shouldn't be squandered or thrown aside. We all have innate wisdom and goodness; this life provides extraordinary opportunities, great and small, to be wise and virtuous. When we keep this in mind at every moment, we turn toward truth.

Consider your own life; think about the many opportunities you have to be true to yourself and what you know is important. Think about ways you can deepen your commitment to those values you hold most dear. Each day as you reflect on this, try to reinforce and firm up your intentions and bring them into action. Take some practical steps in this direction, no matter how small. Take this contemplation into action.

II

LIFE IS SHORT; THERE IS NO TIME TO WASTE.

Recently I was visiting friends, and their children were watching a videotape of *The Wizard of Oz* with Judy Garland. I think we've probably all seen the movie. Judy Garland was an enchanting, multitalented girl, and on screen she remains breathtakingly young. Of course, she died almost twenty years ago, but in this classic film she is frozen in time. Whenever I look at this movie, I find it hard to believe that Judy Garland is no longer a fresh-faced preadolescent belting out 'Somewhere over the Rainbow.' But she's not. Like everyone, she had problems, grew older, and died. In my own life, it seems like yesterday that I watched the movie for the first time as a young child.

How about you? Don't you have trouble believing the speed with which things pass? One moment you're in high school worrying about which college to attend, and almost the next thing you know you're a full-fledged adult with adult concerns, belief systems, responsibilities, and travails. How does this happen? Is it really true that each of us will grow up, mature, grow old, and die? Sometimes it seems so inconceivable that we choose not to think about it, but we become wiser when we accept the tenuous, short-lived nature of life. Myself, I know I am going to die, but if I am totally honest with myself, I find it hard to believe.

The Buddha told his disciples and followers to think about death and the remembrance of mortality/impermanence. He said that death was his greatest teacher. He told people that remembering how little time we have in this lifetime would help us spend our days on earth more wisely. Reflecting upon death is not meant to be a morbid practice. In fact, it can have the opposite effect; it can help ground us in the *here and now* and make us appreciate the wonderful miracle of life each moment as it's given to us now. The Buddha said:

'The universe and its inhabitants are as ephemeral as the
  clouds in the sky;
Beings being born and dying are like a spectacular dance
  or drama show.
The duration of our lives is like a flash of lightning
  or a firefly's brief twinkle;
Everything passes like the flowing waters of a steep waterfall.'

III

THE JOURNEY THROUGH LIFE ISN'T SUPPOSED TO BE EASY; IT'S SUPPOSED TO BE REAL.

Here's a fact of life: Nobody gets away scot-free. In every life, we are destined to find some disappointment, dissatisfaction, pain, and illness. We are bound to feel confused, insecure, and anxious. The Buddha termed our passage on this earth and the cycle of birth and death that we all experience as 'samsara.' The word in Sanskrit is literally translated as 'journeying,' or cycling and recycling.

Regularly contemplating the travails of our journey helps us to stay realistic about what life is and isn't. Don't be depressed by these thoughts. Instead recognize the joys that can be found by staying grounded and real. Every dip and rise, every twist and turn is part of the infinite journey; why turn aside from any of it?

Too many of us resist authenticity, preferring instead an airbrushed approach to the world. This is easy to do since we live in a time where our values and our vision of reality are influenced and shaped by images that are unreal and false. We watch popular television shows, and we come away thinking that everyone is supposed to be young, beautiful, thin, and rich. We have a false view of a world created by jaded Hollywood values. We create fantasies for ourselves based on what we see and read in contemporary entertainment media or what I call 'airbrush reality.' Too much airbrush reality on a day-to-day basis and we become airheads.

Reflect on the frustrations, joys, and sorrows of a real life. When you are sitting around with nothing to do, and your mind wanders, try to keep it from getting caught up in fantasies of perfection. Don't get caught up in the sizzle; instead, focus on substance and reality. It is right before you, this very moment; don't overlook it.

IV

OUR KARMA IS THE ONE THING WE CARRY WITH US ALWAYS.

As we become more and more conscious, heart-centered, and spiritually awake, we begin to better see how everything we do shapes and creates our destiny. Reflect on the laws of karma and the patterns that have unfolded in your own experience. Reflect on the passages and transitions – the bardos – of your life. My Tibetan teachers often told me that when we die, the only thing we can take with us is our karma. We each have our own personal karmic bank account.

Thinking about your karma helps you face the truth about your own experience; it helps you make changes when necessary. We all do and say things that don't work to make us happy. What about you? Focus on ways you can change and improve your karma. Don't think about changing anybody else's behavior – just your own. What can you do today to change the way you feel tomorrow? Keep your plans manageable and doable within the next 24 hours. Ask yourself the following questions:

Can I improve my attitude toward one person or situation in my life?

Can I let go and be less attached to a situation or thing that is causing me pain?

Can I let go of some negative feelings and cultivate a more positive, loving attitude toward the people in my life who make me angry?

Can I do something today that will help the planet?

He who understands karma understands Dharma and realizes reality.

The Buddha said:

> *'Wherever we go, wherever we remain,*
> *the results of our actions follow us.'*

CHAPTER TWO

Awakening to a Deeper Love –
A Buddha's Love

I went to my first meditation course in Bodh-Gaya, the village in India that has grown up around the tree under which the Buddha attained enlightenment . . . out of curiosity someone asked me, 'Why are you practicing meditation?' The first thing that came to my mind was an image of the Buddha in the main temple near the Bodhi tree, and I found myself saying, 'I'm practicing so that I can have the love of a Buddha, so I can love people the way the Buddha did.'

— From *A Heart as Wide as the World*
by Sharon Salzberg

We all want and need love. In fact, most of us are almost constantly seeking it – often more than anything else in life. That's because like seeks like, and we *are* love. We all have hearts of love. We are the energy of love, like the invisible God's visible body of love, or Buddha's body of love manifesting in this world. It happens through us. Love is not just something we do or experience. Love is a way of being – our most beautiful and unobstructed way of being. It is our truest and deepest calling.

The central theme of Mahayana Buddhism revolves around how we can answer that call by opening our hearts and learning to love and care for others, as well as ourselves. Buddhism teaches us how to transform ourselves so that we will be able to love as purely, unselfishly, and unconditionally as the Buddha loved. Many seekers are highly drawn to this lofty noble goal. However, finding a way to embody this kind of love amidst all the stresses and strains of our daily lives is a monumental challenge. It is far easier said than done! Yet do it we must, and I believe we shall. For love is our true purpose, our true calling. Love is calling each of us home, to the vast reservoir of love within ourselves.

THE SUBTLETIES OF LOVE

Last Sunday, as Marla drove home from a weekend spiritual retreat, she felt highly motivated to do good and be good. It had been an inspiring weekend, and she had been particularly moved by a loving-kindness practice that she found extraordinarily powerful. For her entire life, Marla has been concerned with wanting to help others. The retreat reawakened Marla's commitment to live a more compassionate, caring, and loving life; she wants to apply these feelings to every issue in her life.

Only a week has gone by since Marla returned from the retreat, yet she is already feeling discouraged and disturbed by the difficulties involved in maintaining a consistently loving, unselfish attitude. This morning, for example, Marla was trying to be more loving and caring with her significant other, but Robert was being undeniably self-centered, thinking only of himself as he rushed off early – as always – to play tennis with a client, while she was left to clean up a messy house and buy food for the rest of the weekend. Meanwhile, Marla has stuff of her own she wants to do. She wants to go to the gym; she wants to meditate; she wants to read a book; and she also has some work she brought home to read.

But first she must finish her chores, so Marla forces herself to let go of her resentment against Robert as she resolutely heads off to the store. Later, when Marla returns, staggering into the house with the bundles, the first thing that happens is that a lonely, talkative friend calls to ask for some advice. Marla wants to be available and open to help others so she stays on the phone and listens for a full forty-five minutes. Marla no sooner hangs up when a close friend, Jackie, calls to say that her car 'died.' Could Marla please pick her up at the gas station and drive her home? Jackie is her friend. *If I don't help her,* Marla thinks to herself, *who will I help?*

Marla is backing her car out of the driveway when her sister Pam pulls up. Pam is in tears because she and her husband Chuck have just had another major fight about money; they have scheduled an emergency counseling session. Could Marla please take the baby, and could she also loan them $200 to pay the phone bill because the phone has been turned off because Chuck didn't pay it. Marla loves her sister, and she wants to help, but Pam takes total advantage. *This happens all the time,* Marla thinks. *She just arrives with her problems and I'm supposed to fix them.* More than anything else Marla wants to do good; she wants to be a good sister and a good person. But isn't this all a bit much? As much as Marla wants to be open, caring, and accepting, all she is feeling is put upon. She hasn't even had time to get all her groceries out of the bag, but she is already as busy as a small social service agency.

We all want to be good people. Spiritual seekers particularly are very likely to aspire to be more loving and less selfish. But what does it mean to be loving? What does it mean to be kind and giving? How do we know that we are giving the right things at the right time? Where and when do we draw the line? Is Marla, for example, helping Robert or their relationship by assuming most of the household chores? Is she helping her sister, or is she encouraging dependency? Is she showing love or co-dependence?

So the question remains, what is compassion? What is love? Jesus taught his disciples to give unstintingly. Buddhists are taught that the Buddha gave all he had without holding back. There are numerous teachings about the many previous lifetimes that the Buddha told his followers he remembered. There is an ancient legend that in one of these lifetimes the Buddha was a prince. One day, while he was still a young man, the prince went out for a walk; he looked down a ravine and saw a starving tigress and her cubs. The prince was so pained by the suffering of these animals that he threw himself down into the ravine in order to provide the animals with food. This was an extraordinary act of self-sacrifice. Are any of us capable of this kind of love? Would we want to be? Is this a true story, showing the depth of love that a completely unselfish person can feel, or is it merely a romanticized legend? Of course we don't know. Still, the point is there. Myths can contain greater truths than mere fact.

Love is very simple, but it has many subtleties. The great Indian poet and mystic Kabir, born in the mid-fifteenth century, devoted his life to writing poems and songs of love for God. He sang, 'Subtle is the path of love.' Love has so many mysteries. Love makes us lessen our selfish and self-centered view of the world. The thing about loving someone or something else is that it absolutely teaches and challenges us to go beyond ourselves. Often this is only temporary, but knowing what this feels like if only for a moment gives us a hint of what it means to truly love. Parents the world over know firsthand what it feels like to regard another as more important than one's self. This is one of the great lessons of parenthood.

Yet for all of us, many are the errors in judgment committed in the name of love. Who would argue that many of our sufferings are due to romantic attachments? There are times when we believe we are being loving, while everyone else thinks we are being self-indulgent, co-dependent, and even delusional. Our need for romance, passion, and love often gets corrupted by greed, jealousy, fear, and the shadows of our personal histories.

If we are not conscious and awake, an unrealistic search for romantic love can rule our lives – often at the cost of our happiness and fulfillment. Yet romantic love serves a purpose. Not only can it give us heartache and heartbreak, it can also be like open heart surgery – transporting us beyond ourselves and opening realms of giving, caring, and sharing. It allows us to experience a oneness that is far beyond any mental construct or imagination. It is a personal way to experience oneness – a gateway that can lead us beyond ourselves. Romantic love can be a revelation of what is possible. This is the value of interpersonal relationships and friendships. In many ways, romantic love can be a training and an opening to the experiencing of a greater, more divine love.

In the practical world we inhabit, love often calls for appropriate compromises and boundaries; we need to learn give and take, and we need to stay connected to nitty-gritty reality. My friend and mentor, Ram Dass, used to point out that transpersonal love and nonattachment doesn't mean non-caring. In relationships, we need to strive and sometimes even fight to make them work, and not pretend it doesn't matter. Ram Dass would always say, 'Hold on tight; let go light.' We have to try to make wholesome attempts to make things work, and accept it when they don't.

Love also requires honesty and self-examination. As spiritual seekers, travelling the path of self-discovery, we always have to question our motivations and our reasons for loving. When Marla, for example, goes out of her way for her sister Pam, is she being truly helpful and giving or is she trying to win points in the 'sibling war' by pointing out to her parents that she is the 'good' sister? This is a question Marla has to ask herself.

Questions about love, compassion, and giving are part of what we all have to explore for ourselves as we walk the path of awakening. As seekers, we have to search inward and take a long hard look at our motivations and intentions as we decide what to give, when to give it, and to whom we give it.

One of my first teachers was the late great wandering Hindu holy man, Neem Karoli Baba, whom we all called Maharaji. Maharaji was famous for wearing disguises and showing up where he was least expected. One day in Allahabad, India, dressed as a tattered beggar, he appeared at the back door of one of his longtime disciples, who was a prominent and learned professor of economics – and he asked for food. The professor's sister, who answered the door, shooed him away by banging on pots and pans.

The very next day, Maharaji returned to the household, this time dressed recognizably as the blanket-wrapped swami whom they all loved and adored. As to be expected, the family provided the very best vegetarian feast before Maharaji wandered off on his way. When next the professor came to pay homage at his guru's feet, he had his entire family with him. This time it was Maharaji who shooed *them* away by banging on pots and pans. The householder was deeply shocked and upset so he later returned, this time alone, to ask the guru what had happened and why; he begged forgiveness for anything that he had done wrong. Maharaji told him, 'You never know who comes from God. When I came as a beggar, your sister drove me away, banging pots and pans like I was a mongrel dog. When I came as a guru, you fed me like a king.' The message, of course, is that we should treat everyone as though he or she is a child of God and has been sent by divine will.

This story bothered me for years and made me think deeply about the distinctions I make between people; it made me reflect on my own biases, prejudices, and partiality – and my capacity to give unconditionally and indiscriminately. I am the child of parents who were products of the Great Depression. In our house a greater value was placed on saving than there was on spending. I'm just now starting to experience the joy of giving and spending without reservation, and I've had to ask myself many questions about my feelings about giving. Why, for example, is it sometimes so much easier to give in situations where there is some status connected to the cause or charity? Why do we tend to blot out and erase from our minds the truly needy and the poorest of the poor as though they don't exist, while we cheerfully send beautifully wrapped birthday, Hanukkah, birthday, and Christmas gifts to people who already have much more than they need? We all do it, don't we? Often we don't even really see the needy street people we pass by when we are going to visit someone; sometimes we are carrying expensive house gifts – wine and flowers. We bring such gifts because we want to give a nice present but also because we want people to think we have great taste, or we want to be invited back. But sometimes we need to ask ourselves how much of this is true giving and how much is self-serving. Motivation is what is most relevant.

In Thailand, where the monks go out each morning to collect alms, they pass anonymously from house to house. In Japan, the monks wear large straw basket hats to cover their faces so the giver never knows who is the recipient of their generosity. This practice emphasizes the transcendental, self-less nature of generosity. That's the thing about giving in all its forms: It extends transpersonally and anonymously throughout the universe. We smile at a stranger; the stranger feels happier about the world and extends his good feeling to someone else, who in turn may pass it on. 'Passing it on' is the operative term.

Several years ago, a forest fire swept the parched mountains in northern New Mexico, destroying everything in its path. Completely razed by this wildfire was the Lama Foundation, a community established outside of Taos thirty-five years ago. The Lama Foundation, which was the first East-West spiritual community of its kind in America, is located on the western slopes of Taos Mountain. This large mountain has long been held sacred by the Native Americans of the region. I have taught and led retreats there on several occasions; the disaster was a loss to all of us.

One of my friends at the Lama Foundation was particularly known for her great collection of spiritual books, handicrafts, medicine wheels, statuettes, god's eyes, and works of art – some original, many collected. We all knew how much she loved and was attached to her collection. After the fire she told me that the only pieces of her priceless, lifelong collection that had survived were the ones she had given away. This was, she said, her lesson in nonattachment and the virtue of open-handed generosity. She was glad that she knew where some of her things still remained. All that was left of her lifelong passion was what she had given to others.

GIVING MEANING TO LIFE

In Buddhism, the most loving and glorious spiritual ideal is that of the Bodhisattva, the spiritual warrior whose purpose in life is to help others find enlightenment, liberation, and truth. The Bodhisattva Vow of Mahayana Buddhism is very simple:

Sentient beings are numberless; I vow to liberate them.
Delusions are inexhaustible; I vow to transcend them.
Dharma teachings are boundless; I vow to master them.
The Buddha's enlightened way is unsurpassable; I vow to embody it.
For the ultimate benefit of all beings without exception, throughout
this and all my lifetimes, I dedicate myself to the practice and
realization of enlightenment until all together reach that goal.

Within the last twenty or thirty years, many of the great Asian teachers of their time have welcomed Western students by sharing with them the Dharma (as the Buddhist teachings of truth are known). Some of us first learned of the Bodhisattva Vow in Asia; many more learned of it in their own countries. The Dalai Lama himself has come to this country and given this vow to thousands of men and women. In Darjeeling in the early autumn of 1973, I first took the vow with my late teacher, Kalu Rinpoche. New students would sometimes ask him if they could take the Bodhisattva Vow more than once. He would tell them to take it all the time – every morning as well as every night. The Bodhisattva Vow is a living vow that we reaffirm every day, not just once in a lifetime. Kalu Rinpoche would encourage us to take refuge in the Bodhisattva Vow, explaining that taking refuge in the Vow was taking refuge and solace in our higher aspirations. In this way we relied upon the profound power of pure intention to transform our words, thoughts, and deeds.

The Bodhisattva ideal represents ultimate love – divine compassion translated into human form. With this kind of unconditional love, we consistently consider the well-being of everyone. Anything we unselfishly do for others has implications and repercussions. By making this level of commitment, we recognize that there are consequences to our actions; everything we do and say affects others. In this way, all of our connections become more meaningful. Every encounter counts.

As the Dalai Lama points out, the words don't really matter; whether you call it compassion, love, or charity, the good heart – the heart of unconditional love and unselfish caring – is universal. Whether it is Christ or Buddha, both are brothers-in-truth, driven by the awakened and loving heart of the Bodhisattva. This cosmic principle dwells in each of us. Committing ourselves to cultivating the awakened heart of the Bodhisattva is the greatest service we can dedicate to the world. The Bodhisattva is the ultimate social activist working to alleviate universal suffering throughout all of his or her lifetimes. I call this spiritual activism.

So many people go through their days feeling as though their lives are meaningless and without purpose. However, when we commit ourselves to Bodhisattva practices and the deeper love, selfless service, and boundless compassion these practices entail, by definition we endow our lives with meaning. Caring for the spiritual welfare – the most profound well-being – of others puts our lives in context. This is a reason to get up every morning. Sometimes it may feel as though we are engaged in the exhausting task of putting small drops into large buckets, but we all know that if there are enough drops, eventually the bucket *will* become full. This is a way to give your life richness and purpose.

One of the most popular Mahayana scriptures is the Avatamsaka Sutra, affectionately known as the Flower Garland Sutra. The basic teaching of this sutra is that everything is interwoven, interconnected, and mutually interpenetrating. Reading it, we think of the world as the jeweled lattice of the Hindu God Indra's web, in which each sparkling, mirrorlike jewel reflects and thus contains all the others. Like these reflecting jewels, we are not separate, and we are not one; rather we are interrelated and interconnected. This totality approach to connectedness is what the venerable and loving Vietnamese monk Thich Nhat Hanh calls 'inter-being.' From the light that is reflected from this vast, sacred web of interbeing-ness, we can see that we are all perfect beings perfectly evolving to a natural perfection that is beyond the limiting dualism of perfect and imperfect. Our spiritual journey is recognized, with all its ups and downs, as a perfect unfolding – an unfolding in the light, and of the light.

Before his own fully perfect enlightenment, the Buddha was just like each of us – a seeker striving for freedom and awakening. The Garland Sutra describes the Buddha's spiritual path, telling how in earlier lifetimes as a Bodhisattva he sowed the seeds of awakening in his own heart and mind through compassionate, selfless acts. In this way he cultivated what Buddhists call 'Bodhicitta,' a Sanskrit word that means the awakened heart-mind or the mind of enlightenment. Bodhicitta is the Buddha's heart in each of us.

When Buddhist scholars talk about Bodhicitta, they often make a distinction between two forms, which are known as (1) relative Bodhicitta and (2) absolute Bodhicitta. Relative Bodhicitta refers to the compassionate intention to attain enlightenment and liberation for the benefit of all beings. Absolute Bodhicitta (or the absolute mind of enlightenment) refers to an understanding of the central Buddhist theme of emptiness. Thus the Bodhisattva with the awakened heart-mind of enlightenment (1) strives to attain liberation for all beings and (2) realizes that the true nature of the world is emptiness, infinite openness, or sunyata.

The actual name of the Garland Sutra is the Buddha-vatamsaka Sutra. When people hear the name Garland Sutra, they often think of a garland of flowers, but what this name really represents is a Garland of Buddhas. This image addresses an underlying theme of Mahayana Buddhism: The Mahayana sutras say that when we look at anything, even into the palm of our hand, we can find these infinite Buddha Fields, teeming with enlightened ones. Whether we are staring at the infinite realms of space or at the smallest molecule, what we are seeing are infinite, luminous Buddhas. Whether we are standing in the grandest cathedral or sky gazing through the highest redwoods, we see Buddha Fields without limits, veritable galaxies of Buddha light. Everywhere we look are multitudes – millions and millions of tiny Buddhas. In short, everything is permeated by Buddha-nature – or, if you prefer, by the mind of the Divine. Buddha-nature here, Buddha-nature there, Buddha-nature everywhere.

That's why the gentle spiritual warrior, known as the Bodhisattva, has limitless patience, perseverance, and courage. The Bodhisattva recognizes that no one is totally apart or separate from sacred Buddha-nature. As we strive for enlightenment and the fully realized heart mind, we begin to see that even the smallest kind word, or gentle loving gesture, has repercussions in the infinite Buddha Field we all inhabit. Karmically speaking, everything matters, everything counts, and everything is interconnected. Nothing is ever overlooked by the lord/law of karma. Knowing this lends meaning and purpose to our lives. Each of us totally matters.

I live in the countryside, and often when I am out walking I am struck by the country practice of waving. Car after car passes me on the road; the occupants wave and smile. I wave and smile back. Whether we think about it or not, this little practice of waving on a country road is a way of building spiritual connections and spreading love. Don't we feel good about the mini-relationships we build with our little waves? *How nice and kind that family looked smiling at me. How lovely the kids in the station wagon seem with their faces pressed against the back window, waving and smiling.* Even the family dog is waving his tail. We feel seen and acknowledged by these little rituals; we feel connected to our fellow travellers.

The great Indian sage Shantideva, whose name means the 'Gentle Master,' lived in the 7th and 8th century. He spent his life teaching others how to see the equality of self and other, and to act from this belief. He said that if you raise even *one* hand in a gesture of reverence to anything or anyone, all the Buddhas clap, rejoice, and rain down blessings. Shantideva lived in a world where people regularly put two hands together and bowed. Yet he taught that even one hand could make a difference. In a practical sense, raising a hand in reverence means that we must put down our weapons. After all, it's difficult to harm or manipulate someone when you are bowing to them. Think of this the next time you feel anger or enmity. Soften yourself by trying to experience a feeling, a glimmer, of reverence for the person who is arousing your ire. In this way we delight the ever-present Buddhas, the great accomplished Bodhisattvas – all the immortals, saints, sages, and protectors of truth and Dharma.

CHAPTER THREE

Connecting to Your
Life Experience

It's never too late to be what you might have been.
– George Eliot

I have a sane and reliable friend who swears that she remembers coming home from the hospital right after being born; her mother wrapped her in a hand-crocheted pink blanket, and placed her in a crib. From that vantage point, she says she witnessed an argument between her two older sisters, one of whom angrily threw a toy doll at my friend, the new baby. My friend has no other childhood memories until she is a bit older, but when she talked to her parents about the pink blanket and the kind of doll that was thrown at her – a bride doll – they confirmed the specifics about the argument she remembered seeing and hearing. I'm not making this up! My friend says that she also remembers talking to 'voices' at the time, saying that she wasn't sure if she was in the right place and whether she was going to be able to deal with her sisters. 'I don't know about this,' she remembers saying. 'This situation may be a little too over-whelming. I think I made a mistake.'

Do you ever look at your life and wonder, did I choose this? Am I at the right address? Am I in the right relationship, the right job? How did I get here anyway? *The Tibetan Book of the Dead* explicitly teaches that we all choose our parents and the lives we lead, even if we are not as conscious about it as someone like, for example, the Dalai Lama. Some religious traditions say that this is the life that was given to us. Buddhism teaches that this is the life we chose, although not entirely consciously. The challenges we face are the challenges we chose to face. This is how we learn; this is how we grow; this is how we become more enlightened.

If that is the case, then it stands to reason that the first lesson we all need to learn is to accept and connect to the lives we are leading. For THIS IS IT. This is the path for us, and the right one. Let's make the most of it. This is the spiritual Way.

THIS IS IT. JUST THIS, HERE NOW.

There is an old Tibetan saying: 'Life runs out while we are preparing to live.' Even in antiquity, when life must have been somewhat slower and simpler, the sage Tibetan masters of the past recognized how easy it is to live in fantasies about the future or a time when everything will be the way we want it to be. But this fantasy-driven approach is neither productive nor ultimately satisfying. Probably one of the first lessons on the spiritual path has to do with an understanding that *this is it*. This is our chance to be happy and do good. I have been in churches that began services with the congregation singing, 'Thank you for the life we are given and the song we sing today.' This reality is our life. This is our song – my song and your song. This vivid song sings through us, right now.

I remember an old story about an elderly Jewish man named Itzhak. Itzhak had spent his life trying to be a good person who honored the commandments and did good deeds. Nonetheless shortly before his death, Itzhak begins worrying about the reception he will get from God in the afterlife. He worries that he has been a failure and that he will be compared to the prophets of old and asked questions like:

Were you as good a leader as Moses?

Were you as wise as Solomon?

Did you have the vision of Isaiah?

When Itzhak finally dies and goes to meet God, he is still worrying about whether he lived up to his Lord's expectations and comparisons that might be made. With great trepidation, he waits to see which questions he will be asked. And they astonish him.

Did you have the wisdom of Itzhak?

Did you have the vision of Itzhak?

Were you genuinely and authentically yourself?

This is *your* life. Right here. Right now. Just this. Your life is your very own path. Don't wish for someone else's; instead search for ways to be like your own true self and fulfill all your own promise and possibility. You are the spiritual treasure you are trying to discover and reveal. The love and the challenges you receive from your friends, your mates, your family, and your work are all part of the process of your awakening – all grist for the mill. You are 'the jewel in the lotus,' as Tibetans sing in the favorite mantra, **'Om Mani Pedmé Hung.'** You are the beautiful blossoming, the inner treasure.

CONNECTING TO THE LESSONS
IN YOUR OWN LIFE

Why do so many things in life go right? Why do so many others go wrong?

Why is it that so often when we look at our lives we wonder, 'Why me?' or 'Why is this happening?' yet when we look at someone else, we can clearly see cause and effect at work. For example:

✳ Last October my friend Meryl began to feel so exhausted that, as she put it, she didn't have the strength to get out of bed every morning. She had been fine the previous summer, following her usual daily routine. Until she began to feel tired, this was Meryl's weekday schedule:

6:00 A.M. Wake up, dress quickly, jog to gym
6:45–7:45 Work out
7:45–9:00 Jog back home, shower, dress, go to work
9:00–12:30 Work
12:30–2:00 Business lunch

2:00–6:30 Work
6:30–11:00 Work-related or social activity
11:00–11:30 Watch nightly news
11:30–12:00 Read work-related papers and material
12:00 Prepare for bed and lights out

When Meryl first began to complain of exhaustion, she started taking more vitamins, but they didn't do any good. Then she started cutting out some of her nightly activities, and began getting to bed by 10:00 and watching sitcoms until she fell asleep. That still didn't work. She began to wonder whether she needed to increase her strength training at the gym, but when she attempted to do that, she started to feel even more weary. Finally she went to the doctor, who after many tests, diagnosed chronic fatigue syndrome. *Why,* she keeps asking herself, *did I get sick?*

✳ Robert, who owns a small printing business, wants to know why he can never find a production assistant with whom he gets along. Robert likes being around highly educated people who challenge him, so inevitably everybody he hires is argumentative, overqualified, and ill-suited for a job that requires production and organizing skills. Inevitably his employees stay with him for no more than six months. All of them seem to have a difficult time understanding what Robert wants his assistant to do. Some of them become frustrated and annoyed and quit in a huff; others are more polite, giving adequate notice before leaving. More than one has simply left the office at lunchtime and not returned.

What is going wrong here, Robert asks. *Is it me? Is it them? Is it the work?*

✳   About a year ago, Maria went into an animal shelter and adopted Gertrude, a large black and tan dog of indeterminate lineage. A few months later she was standing on a street corner with Gertrude, waiting for a light to change. A loud noise startled the dog, who broke free and bolted in the opposite direction even though Maria had been holding the leash. Ted, a man who was standing at the same corner, instinctively used his foot to step down on the dog's leash, stopping Gertrude's escape. Today Maria and Ted are deeply in love and planning a wedding next year. They both often ask each other, 'How did this happen?' 'Is this a miracle, or what?' 'How did we get so lucky?'

Heard at Logan Airport terminal in Boston: 'Unattended baggage may be lost or confiscated.' Isn't that how it goes in life itself when we fail to attend to our baggage? Recently I was in Chicago teaching a five-day retreat. When I returned home and walked through the door, I smelled something strange – something damp and mildewed, like a musty old swamp, actually. What could it be? Something made me look down in the basement, and what to my wondering eyes should appear but about two or three inches of water.

I put on my boots, and waded down into the basement to assess the damage. Ruined were several boxes of winter gear and some packing material. What didn't get ruined were my file cabinets which were all raised on cement blocks a few inches off the ground.

Why did my basement get flooded? Why were some of my things ruined and others saved? Well first of all, the basement of my old farmhouse, which has stood in a field for more than a hundred years, has no drain. Secondly, I didn't notice that the water heater was beginning to leak. Oops! Water heaters typically only last from five to ten years. I had even had some indications that mine was failing because for months it had been making funny noises that I chose to ignore.

As a Buddhist, I don't believe in accidents, and yet I don't pretend to understand how all things fit together. This is part of the mystery of life with all its crazy connections and disconnections. Recently while walking down a Manhattan street, I ran into an old friend I hadn't seen in twenty years. Why were we both standing on a corner near Bloomingdale's on the same day, waiting for a light to change? Who can explain synchronicity? Yet we know it exists.

When I was growing up, many of the mothers of my friends were home watching television in the middle of the afternoon. They were addicted to soap operas. I never really watched one from start to finish, but I remember stopping in a friend's family room and asking someone else's mom what was the plotline in the show she was watching. She told me. About a year later, I was once again in my friend's home, and once again I asked his mother what was going on. I was astonished that the main characters were embroiled in the same kinds of situations. The 'good guys' were still putting themselves at emotional and physical risk and the resident 'bitch' was still making the same people unhappy. *Wow,* I remember thinking, *don't these people ever learn?*

When most of us stop long enough and really take the time to reflect on what we experience – good and bad – we can't help but see patterns emerging. We see how often we are careless in thought, word, and deed; we see how we have sometimes been appropriately open and caring, and we also see the times we have been determinedly argumentative and defensive.

Our lives with all their 'accidents' and synchronistic happenings provide us with dozens of opportunities to learn from our experiences. The question is, Do we garner the insights and lessons we need through these experiences? Do we learn which behaviors give us joy and which cause us pain? Do we pay attention, or do we go on unconsciously year after year wondering *Why is this happening to me?* Are we like sleepwalkers dreaming our way along on a treadmill of our own unconscious making?

Karma is a very pragmatic explanation of cause and effect. We polish a piece of silver and we see the shine; we plant some seeds, and we grow our own salad; we help a friend, and we are rewarded with friendship. Right now, we can all ask ourselves, What are the paybacks in our own lives? Is what we do and say getting us what we want and need? What changes could we make in our own attitudes and actions that might produce positive effects? Do we need to become more measured and less driven? Do we need to be more open and less guarded? Do we need to be more giving and less demanding?

Enlightenment is about seeing clearly how things work; it's about knowing and understanding what is; it's about connecting to the truth of the present moment. What better place to apply ourselves to reality as it presents itself to us than in our daily moment-by-moment lives?

PAYING ATTENTION TO WHAT'S HAPPENING, AS IT HAPPENS

In everybody's life there are subterranean parts that are not getting our full attention – parts that we are sweeping under the rug and choosing to ignore. They may be skeletons – or unattended baggage – in our psychological closets. Sometimes these parts are material, as in my basement; often they are less tangible. Often there are sounds emanating from these areas – not necessarily sirens or fire alarms, but sounds nonetheless. Most of us have had the experience of being in relationships with people who are making 'noises,' letting us know in dozens of small ways that they are dissatisfied or unhappy. Parents of teenagers have told me that they don't need to go to a school conference to find out whether or not their children are doing well; they can read success or failure in the way a child opens and closes the door when they come home from school.

As we become more enlightened, wiser, and more spiritually intelligent about our lives, we learn to listen more closely to the messages we are receiving about how we lead our lives. We learn to hear the noises around us warning us off or cheering us on. We learn to question our own motivations and behavior. When we practice clear seeing, it becomes apparent that we need to deal realistically with the lives we have created and the people and situations around us; when we practice wisdom, it is obvious that we need to look at the world and our individual lives without any delusions or distortions.

Walking down the street one day I saw someone wearing a T-shirt that read, *'Denial is not just the name of a river in Egypt.'* This made me laugh. Denial is an operative force in all our lives. We see what we are conditioned to seeing; we see what we want to see. When something happens that doesn't mesh with our version of reality, often the first response is to deny that it's taking place.

The Buddha encouraged us to look at life neither pessimistically nor optimistically, but *realistically*. Of course this is easier said than done. Whether we are examining our relationships with family, friends, coworkers, lovers, or mates, we all tend to look at the world from our own vantage point, instead of seeing the truth of what's in front of us. Many people remember the movie *Rashomon* where the same event is viewed from several different points of view. The Rashomon effect is operative all around us, all the time. I have a friend who lives in Boston; in July he was upset because he was forced to spend a summer weekend in his air-conditioned apartment instead of on a New England beach as he had planned. He felt deprived. To most of the world's population, he spent an almost idyllic weekend in perfect comfort; to him, it was as if he had been imprisoned.

We also tend to see different things even when we are in the same room. I once knew somebody who was phobic about dead birds. She lived in Manhattan. 'Where,' I asked her with amazement, 'do you see dead birds?' 'Take a walk with me,' she replied, 'and you'll see that there are dead birds everywhere.' One day I did just that. As we walked, she pointed them out: dead pigeons and sparrows, hidden under cars and in alleyways. I certainly would not have noticed them if I were alone. They did seem to be everywhere. My friend had made an obsession about spotting the dead bodies, and a phobia out of that obsession. We project our karmic perceptions, and it defines and colors our experience.

In Buddhism we learn that our experiences – what we see, what we think, and what we feel – have to do with our own attachments, perceptions, and interpretations. It's all a matter of perspective. Thus we construct our reality.

UNDERSTANDING SAMSKARAS

Not that long ago, a man attended one of my lectures with his wife and her twin sister. The two women were remarkably identical. While they were standing there, an older woman became engaged in a conversation with the three of them and couldn't resist asking the man a question that he must hear with great regularity. 'How do you tell them apart?' The man's reply was interesting. 'They don't look at all alike to me,' he said. 'In fact, when I met my wife, she was with her sister. I was so attracted to my wife that I didn't pay much attention to her sister or even notice the resemblance.'

For this man, when his wife walked across the stage of his life, everything clicked, and all of his antennae shot up. Why is that? Why does one person appeal to us so much more than another? Why do we choose the friends we do? Why do we gravitate toward certain occupations? Why do we find some events appealing and others completely boring? What a mystery! And yet if we look more deeply, certain patterns emerge.

There is an ancient Sanskrit word, *'samskaras,'* which is used to explain this phenomenon. 'Samskara' literally means tendencies or inclinations. In Buddhism the definition is broadened somewhat to mean 'impulses,' or 'tendencies to make certain choices because of karmic imprinting.' In modern parlance, we sometimes hear people use expressions like 'whatever floats your boat.' This conveys the same sense as a samskara. My friend Barry often complains about his mother, saying, 'She pushes all my buttons.' In short, samskaras are those tendencies we have to respond positively or negatively to certain situations or people. It is deeply ingrained psychological conditioning.

Everything we do, say, think, and feel creates an impression in the mind. Everything we see, hear, smell, and taste creates an impression or impulse. Buddhist teachings say that we are all bundles of samskaras or impulses. Somebody or something pushes these samskara–buttons, and we react.

For example:

✳ When Sarah was a child, she wore a blue dress to go to a county fair with her favorite aunt and uncle. Her uncle gave her a quarter to put on a number at one of the games, and Sarah won a small teddy bear. Since that day, whenever Sarah wears blue, she feels lucky.

✳ When Theo was growing up, he had an older sister whom he resented because she was always telling him what to do. Now that he is a married man, he finds that he often responds to simple requests from his wife in the same way that he responded to his bossy sister.

Think about the dozens of samskara-buttons that reveal themselves in your life every day. We walk past luncheonettes and smell coffee brewing or pancakes being made; we want some. We hear angry noises or spooky music; our adrenaline starts flowing. We see a comfortable-looking couch; we want to sit down. Advertisers, who are in the business of sending us subliminal messages, know all about samskaras. These are the buttons they attempt to push when they want us to buy their products. If they could, they would probably implant more samskaras in us to better manipulate and direct our consumer impulses.

For each of us individually there are hundreds and hundreds of unique samskaras. Some are generational. An eighty-year-old, for example, might respond to big band music in the same way that people of my generation respond to the Beatles or a twenty-year-old reacts to the music of Pearl Jam. Some samskaras are identified with certain countries or ethnic groups, and some are familial. There are many more, of course, that are the result of one's own individual experiences. Often the people we choose as friends and romantic partners instinctively seem to know how to push our samskara-buttons.

Our samskara-buttons help create and perpetuate our karma. In fact ancient Eastern teachings say samskaras form the basis of our many attractions and aversions and therefore are driving forces behind our thoughts and our actions. Teachings about reincarnation or rebirth say that it is the samskaras which attract and repel us and are therefore part of what bring us back time and time again to this world.

When the Buddha realized perfect enlightenment, he was free from his samskaras. Never again would he be at the mercy of his likes or dislikes; he had achieved mastery of his thoughts and feelings, and with that, of course, comes freedom and inner peace.

Understanding what drives us and how our samskara-buttons are pushed helps us understand how our karma is formed. The Tibetans say that all the samskaras that drive us fall into one of eight categories, which they call the Eight Worldly Winds or the Eight Traps. These are paired up in four sets:

* Pleasure and pain

* Loss and gain

* Praise and blame

* Fame and shame

Every single one of us has these eight buttons, each of which is inscribed with these individual names. When anything in our lives pushes one or more of these buttons, we respond:

✳ Elizabeth, for example, is a beautiful woman with a very negative husband who keeps telling her that she has gained weight and is not attractive enough. Intellectually Elizabeth knows that she is attractive, and she knows that her husband is simply being cruel. But because so many of her buttons are being pushed (pain, shame, blame, loss), she loses sight of reality.

✳ Ian, who is having trouble at work, is nearly overcome with fear at the idea that he might lose his job and the status that comes with it. When his buttons are being pushed, he becomes almost irrational.

✳ Margaret believes that she will never be perfectly happy until she can move into a larger house. Just thinking about the tiny, cramped apartment she is living in gives her pain.

All of these people, of course, are allowing their lives to be dominated by the things that push their buttons, and in so doing, they are failing to find joyous freedom and spontaneous expression in the present moment. As we become more and more purified of karma and more enlightened, our samskara reaction buttons lose their hold over us. We find greater and greater freedom from conditioning as well as from unfulfilling patterns, fixations, behaviors, and neuroses; we find ourselves becoming free of illusion and confusion as well as overweening attachment and desire. We become free to be genuinely ourselves moment to moment – free to experience the natural bliss and spontaneity of just *being*. Freedom is in our hands.

CONNECTING TO YOUR INNER SPIRITUAL WARRIOR

Initially we may have a hard time relating to the amount of work that the Buddhist path – or any other genuine spiritual path – encourages. But anyone who has walked the path knows that the greatest battles one faces are internal. The most determined demons are the demons that live within us. I think it is important for all of us to do more than just pay lip service to this idea. People often come to me for counseling about their personal lives, and in these conversations I'm made aware of how much energy and thought we all expend trying to avoid our own problems by focusing on someone else. I've spoken to many women who tell me that their biggest problems in life are caused by a male partner's relationship with his mother, for example, while men may tell me that their biggest problems are created by their partners' workaholism or attitude toward career. When we focus on our partners' weaknesses, we can deny our own karmic patterns, forgetting that it takes two to tangle.

Some of us are consistently drawn to co-dependent relationships; others of us are so enveloped in narcissistic behaviors and judgments that we can't get past our self-referring, self-preoccupied view of the cosmos. The first task of the spiritual warrior is to get honest about his or her own life and feelings. If we are going to walk the spiritual path with the courage and bravery that it and we deserve, then we have to begin facing up to a major truth:

Inside each of us is a core of essential goodness and purity. Wrapped around this core – this Buddha within – are layers of conditioned responses, attitudes, patterns, habits, and obscuring behaviors. Some of these layers reflect the goodness of our basic Buddha-nature; others do not. To fully awaken and reveal the Buddha within, we have to honestly recognize, acknowledge, and deal with the ingrained problematic conditioning that we all have. We must have the inner strength and fortitude to honestly face these parts of ourselves. There is no way around it except through it.

When we talk about becoming awake, we mean becoming fully conscious and aware of what is actually going on with us – and within us. If we're involved in destructive relationships, for example, we need to spend time unraveling why we are repeatedly attracted to these relationships. If we consistently find ourselves in unfulfilling work situations, we need to examine why this keeps happening. If we are abusing our health, we need to recognize what we are doing, and why, as a first vital step toward positive change. This level of consciousness isn't easy to achieve, but it can be done. It requires the honesty, courage, and inspired effort of a true spiritual warrior. It takes guts to open up and soften up to the tendencies, vulnerability, and shadows that abide within us.

As a Buddhist, I strive to live fully in the present moment, the here and now – the Holy Now. When I say that, some people might automatically misunderstand. They assume that living 'in the now' means 'living *for* the now.' Nothing could be further from teachings of Buddhism, which instruct us to 'live in the now' and prepare for the future whether that future is tomorrow or in the next world. The whole teaching of karma is directed at helping seekers improve their lives by altering unsatisfying behavior. In Buddhism, we foster spiritual intelligence by understanding karma and taking the long view.

CONTEMPLATING YOUR LIFE

Self-reflection helps us heal our lives. The first step in any process of change involves facing and accepting the problem that needs changing. Try the following exercise:

Sit down someplace comfortable where you can just be alone with your thoughts. Take a breather. Relax and take a few breaths. Let go of the troubles and trials of the day. Let the tension and internal conflict and friction drain away. Drop everything.

Turn inward. Slow down. Calm down. Give yourself the gift of being with yourself for a time, like a soul admitted to its own private infinity.

Now: Consider for a moment where you are in life and how you got here. Try not to run away from your thoughts.

Now: Consider for just a moment where you would like to be in a month, a year, five years, and ten years. Think about what you would like to have done and accomplished. Think about what it would be like to be on your deathbed. What would you like to look back and see that you have accomplished? What would you like your obituary to say?

Now: Consider what you have become already. Consider who and what you think you are, and what you might like to do or be if you were given the chance and the choice.

Ask yourself – this is a serious question – if someone gave you the cosmic credit card, what would you do with the rest of your life? Please think about it without editing your thoughts. Your answer could be extremely revealing.

What would you really love to do in order to make a life, not just a living? How far from that way of living are you today?

What would you do about your relationships? How would you change the way you are with others?

What would you do with your creativity? The great statesman Benjamin Disraeli once said, 'Most people die with their music still locked up inside of them.' What would you do to unlock your own inner music?

What would you do with your work? Do you do your work as if it matters, or are you just killing time trying to get through the week to the weekend before beginning the whole ratrace all over again?

What would you do about your health? What habits would you change to make yourself more healthy? How would you change your exercise and eating habits to make yourself feel better and be more fit?

What would you do about your spiritual life? Would you join a group of other people who are committed to a more spiritual life? Would you devote some time and energy to private contemplation, meditation, yoga, or prayer?

What would you do with your compassion and concern for the world? Would you find a way to contribute and help others? What would that be?

Ask yourself, Am I living in tune with my own interests, principles, and beliefs? Am I connecting to the sacred in my own life? Do I walk my talk and practice what I preach?

Is my life helping me develop and contribute my special gifts and talents to the world, bringing out the very best in me, and delivering satisfaction and fulfillment?

Is there any other way – perhaps a road less travelled – I could possibly still take and explore?

Ask yourself, Who am I today and who can I be?

How can I get from here to there? What is the way to my highest happiness?

Where is the next step? What is the first step? Shall I take it? What prevents me from taking such a step today?

82

MINDFULNESS IS THE TOOL

The single greatest tool that we can all access to help us connect to our true lives is *paying attention,* or the cultivation of conscious awareness, which Buddhists call 'mindfulness.' Mindfulness is how we connect to the reality of 'what is.' When we are fully mindful, we are vividly aware of precisely what is happening, when it is happening. When we are mindful, we are better able to see the reality of any situation. This is called clear vision. When we are mindful, we have greater mastery over our own lives. When we are mindful, we find greater joy in the small moment-by-moment pleasures of life; we are more fully present, less absentminded. We can savor life and plumb deeper into its depths rather than merely wading in the shallows.

Right now, stop what you are doing, let go of your thoughts; let go of your activities.

Breathe in through your nostrils, counting one . . . Breathe out, counting two.

Breathe in through your nostrils, counting one . . . Breathe out, counting two.

Do this ten times.

Now start again. Breathe in. Breathe out.

Be silent, as the world slows down. Be aware of what is crossing your gaze right now. A butterfly flits by the window. A cat stretches in the sun. A sparrow alights on the tree limb. All this in the space of a few short breaths. Take notice!

✳

Or do this meditation with your eyes closed, becoming totally aware of sounds, like a very sensitive listening station. Enter the present moment totally through the delicious gateway of sound. Sound is a good object of meditation since it exists only in the now.

We meditate in order to train in mindfulness. In fact, the classic, most basic Buddhist meditation is called Mindfulness of Breathing. When the Buddha gave his instructions on mindfulness, he told his students and disciples that as they go through life, they should be aware of four things:

✳ their bodies

✳ their feelings and emotions

✳ their thoughts

✳ events as they occur

When we practice basic Buddhist meditation, which is called Mindfulness of Breathing, what we are doing is training ourselves to be more mindful and attentive in life. When a disciple asked the Buddha what it meant to live with impeccable mindfulness, the Buddha told him that a disciple should act with clear comprehension – clear vision – in walking, standing, eating, drinking, sitting, falling asleep, awakening, speaking, and keeping silent. This pretty much covers it.

The great contemporary Vietnamese peace activist and meditation master Thich Nhat Hanh says, 'You've got to practice meditation when you walk, stand, lie down, sit, and work, while washing your hands, washing the dishes, sweeping the floor, drinking tea, talking to friends, or whatever you are doing.' In other words, all the time. Can any of us afford to sleepwalk through life? Don't we all want to be more fully awake and alive?

Mindfulness is the opposite of mindlessness. Through mindless living, we dissipate our energy, and squander our lives. Through mindful living, we inhabit fully the present moment and connect more totally with whomever we are with and with whatever we are doing. Then the smallest act becomes unimaginably blessed. Mindfulness is like the wish-fulfilling jewel, the Philosopher's Stone, a genuine elixir. Connecting to it, we connect to spiritual gold. Mindful awareness is transformative.

In the hectic world we all inhabit, it seems almost impossible to be mindful all the time. As we commute to work, our minds tend to jump forward to what we're going to do once we arrive. Often we daydream about events that have already taken place. We live in yesterday or tomorrow. This, of course, is the antithesis of mindfulness. When we lose the present moment, we lose our place in life.

CONNECTING TO THE PRESENT MOMENT THROUGH THE POWER OF NOW

Take a breath; take a break. Cultivate the power of the present moment by entering into the holy now.

To do this meditation, just make yourself comfortable. Lie, sit, stand. It doesn't matter.

Breathe in slowly through your nostrils.

As you breathe in, repeat this inner mantra to yourself: 'Just this, here now.'

As you breathe out, repeat again: 'Just this. Here now.' Use this mantra as an inner form of prayer or chant of contemplation and meditation.

Inhale . . . Just this, here now.

Exhale . . . Just this, here now.

There is nothing but this moment. This sacred moment. Just this, here now.

Let everything else subside, and just go with the natural flow of things, left just as they are. Trust it.

There is no greater miracle than this. Just this. Here now.

There is nowhere else to go, nowhere else to be than just this, here now.

This is the moment we've been waiting for. This is the great crossroads of past and future. This is the goal of our journey. Just this, here now.

There is nothing extra to get rid of and nothing missing that we need to find — just this glorious, radiant, abundant here . . . now.

Right here is how we find ourselves, just as we are. Just this.

Right here is where eternity and infinity converge in the present moment. Right here is the gateway to infinity, to the timeless. Just this. Here now.

This is the eternal moment, the mystical instant, the timeless time beyond time and space – yet totally, precisely present. Just this. Here now.

Don't miss it.

CHAPTER FOUR

Developing Authentic Presence

When you meet a person who has inner authentic presence, you find he has an overwhelming genuineness, which might be somewhat frightening because it is so true and honest and real. You experience a sense of command radiating from the person of inner authentic presence . . . This is not just charisma. The person with inner authentic presence has worked on himself and made a thorough and proper journey. He has earned authentic presence by letting go, and by giving up personal comfort and fixed mind.

– Chogyam Trungpa Rinpoche

'Just be yourself.'

How often have we heard these simple words of wisdom? How often have we repeated them? I recently heard a mother counseling her child who was about to go for a preinterview at the college of her choice,

'Bettina, just be yourself.' In Shakespeare's *Hamlet,* Polonius, the wise elder, advises his son, Laertes:

'This above all: to thine own self be true,

And it must follow, as the night the day,

Thou canst not then be false to any man.'

Whether it's couched in Elizabethan English or the current vernacular – as in 'get real' – it's good advice. What a wonderful feeling it is to be able to be authentic – to be real. To just be yourself is easier said than done, is it not? Why do most of us find it difficult to be the men and women we really are?

The hard truth is that while we were growing up the most prevalent message we probably heard was not 'just be yourself.' In fact, most people tell me that the favored instructions of their formative years were 'Do what people expect of you,' or the ever-popular 'Just do what we tell you.' Messages such as these reinforced our own tendencies to create armor and roles for ourselves that primarily reflected societal expectations. Perhaps we exerted more effort in trying to fulfill these expectations than we did in cultivating authentic presence – our genuine, original, unfabricated, and uncontrived beingness in the world.

As we go through life, many of us get so caught up with the roles we play that we lose all sight of or sense of connection with our own authentic nature. We forget who we are. We become who we ain't. In short, the stories we make up about ourselves and others separate us from the truth of who we are; the roles we play create barriers that keep us from genuine spiritual connectedness – either with ourselves or with others.

This is particularly true when we begin to believe our own stories, our own hype about the roles we play, creating false fronts that become hardened and impenetrable; for obvious reasons this level of inauthenticity will almost inevitably cause havoc in our personal lives. Our children and mates, for example, don't always want to relate to the 'great salesman,' 'the big boss,' or the accomplished 'deal maker.' They want to connect with us – the real people behind the masks and costumes. They want us, not our performances. Sometimes we get into playing exhausting domestic roles at home as well. Instead of being ourselves, we begin to act like the moms/dads/husbands/wives we've seen on TV sitcoms; instead of being genuine, we become weary characters from central casting.

If the spiritual quest is the quest for truth, *and it is,* the best place to begin this search is with ourselves. What is our own truth? Who are we? How can we become more authentic and true?

GROUNDED AND REAL

As I was writing this chapter, the airwaves were thick with the sad news of the death of John F. Kennedy, Jr. People around New York City were being interviewed, talking about a man who they had come to know as a neighbor. My friends who live in Manhattan tell me that they often ran into him – at the neighborhood dog run, at local restaurants and coffee shops. Everyone seems to be particularly impressed with one quality: his effort to be a regular guy who lived a normal life, filled with normal, everyday activities. I read an interview with a messenger who had delivered a package to JFK, Jr. The messenger said that his hand was shaking, and Kennedy asked him why. The messenger told him that he felt that Kennedy was a historical figure. Kennedy replied, 'I'm just a person like you.' This touched my heart.

We all love people who are able to stay grounded and real, no matter what their role in life is. This is one of the reasons why so many people love the Dalai Lama. No matter how many international peace prizes and awards he wins, no matter how many world leaders he meets, no matter how many people bow in his presence, he always bows back – in the same way to everyone. He knows that we are all equal in the light of eternity. Fully present for each person he meets, in each moment, the Dalai Lama is an inspiring example of someone with an awakened heart.

The Dalai Lama has cultivated and maintains a sense of authentic presence, and his spiritual energy is awe-inspiring. And yet as he often reminds us, he thinks of himself as a simple monk. As much as possible, he tries to follow that path and live the life of a Buddhist monk. Of course, he's a modern man. He's a diplomat; he loves science. He's very interested in the world around him. He's a human rights activist, who extends his mission to several dozen different nations every year. But he still gets up at 4:00 A.M. every morning, and meditates for two hours before he switches on the BBC World News at 6:00 A.M. He eats breakfast, sees his advisors, and receives visitors from near and far.

One of the Dalai Lama's special qualities is his determination to try to see everyone who wants to meet him. If you went to Dharamsala, in the foothills of Northern India, where he lives, if you were patient, you'd almost certainly get to see him one on one if you tried. He is happy to see everybody. He is especially focused on meeting every single Tibetan who escapes from Tibet.

The Dalai Lama knows who he is. He's just a man. He doesn't think of himself as an exalted spiritual leader. He thinks he's a human being, a guy who has things he wants to do and who does them to the best of his ability; he also has some things that he can't do because he has a big public service job right now. But as he always says, he might prefer to study and meditate, and he will retire to do so when his people can safely live again in their own country of Tibet.

Of course, the Dalai Lama doesn't say, 'I'm just a simple guy.' He says, 'I'm a simple monk.' That's very modest, as the Buddha intended his monks to be. And the Dalai Lama is an exemplary monk. He doesn't think he's a saint, a Nobel Prize laureate, or somebody we should look up to. He just thinks of himself as a monk. He's trained his whole life to be better and better at it. I always think of the Dalai Lama as fulfilling the Jewish ideal of a perfect 'mensch.' It's very mensch-like to know who you are, where you fit in, and that you are like everybody else. The Dalai Lama sounds humble and modest because he is genuinely humble and modest. He's also brilliant, charming, interesting, and extraordinarily present, but when he goes back to his hotel room, he takes off his Hush Puppies and reads or meditates. When he watches TV in his hotel rooms, he channel surfs. Like the Buddha of old, he is an inspiration to all of us because he is able to be such an enlightened human being right here in the world – without being totally overcome by it.

IMAGE ISSUES – A SIGN OF THE TIMES

I spent most of the 1980s in a cloistered Tibetan monastery. But once when I was back in the United States for a short visit, I saw a videotape of 'Saturday Night Live.' My fellow Long Islander, actor Billy Crystal, had created a well-attired character with pomaded hair and a deep tan, who joked that he'd rather 'look good than feel good.' Everyone laughed. Within the last two decades in this country, 'looking good' has been elevated to a virtue. And 'looking good' has come to mean certain things: looking successful, looking well dressed, looking well exercised, looking organized, looking 'together.' Since we live in a world that puts most of its emphasis on style, fashion, and performance, it's small wonder that we spend so much time worrying about image issues. Day in and day out we are bombarded by a host of messages reminding us to wear clothing with the right labels, eat food with the right labels, drive cars with the right make, enjoy the right activities, and have the right kind of kids at the right schools. It's kind of hard to focus on cultivating authentic presence when you are debating the merits of a Toyota over a Grand Cherokee, Ralph Lauren over Calvin Klein, Pepsi over Coke, or the benefits of cosmetic surgery over an expensive vacation.

Just last night I was visiting a friend's house, and I saw a bit of a television sitcom in which one of the main characters, a successful young woman – who has to go to an office party – invites her more economically challenged boyfriend to attend with her, but then, realizing that he doesn't own an appropriate suit for such an event, tries to buy him an expensive outfit similar to the ones her colleagues will be wearing. She wants him to look like everybody else who will be there; otherwise, she worries, he will not fit in – meaning that *she* won't fit in, or look good. It goes without saying that the relationship 'crashed' over this issue.

These kinds of problems aren't limited to TV land. I recently counseled a woman who said that she had met 'the most wonderful man in the world.' She described him as being good, kind, adoring, and smart, but he was, she said, a little too short and she didn't like the way he dressed or the jewelry he wore. I felt far worse for her than for him.

We're all occasionally guilty of choosing our romantic partners and friends based upon the image they project to the world. We make judgments, good and bad, based on what we see on the outside. If someone is driving a Mercedes, we assume she is rich. If someone is carrying a stack of books, we assume he is an intellectual. If someone is walking a dog, we assume she is an animal lover. Yet there is so much more to all of us than what we superficially appear to be.

As a Westerner and a Tibetan lama, I find that people are often confused, and sometimes even disappointed, that I am not wearing maroon and gold robes or talking and behaving in ways that they expect – whatever those might be. For years,

I was a monk who wore saffron robes and had a shaved head. When I left the monastery, it was my Tibetan teachers in fact who encouraged me to be more authentic to my background in terms of dress. 'If you're teaching in America,' they said, 'teach like you're an American.' That advice was first given to me in France by an incarnate lama who said, 'Surya, you could afford to be more authentic.' I think we could all take a page from that lesson book. It took me a while to realize that the authenticity and essence of the Buddha's teachings had nothing to do with traditional Asian dress. I am grateful to my friend the lama who said that to me.

When people hear that I am a Buddhist lama, they also seem to expect that I should be chanting and meditating around the clock. They expect me to play a particular role. A question that I'm often asked, for example, is 'Are you enlightened, Surya?' When people ask me that I sense that what they are really asking is 'Are you perfect?' 'Are you completely blissed out, calm, and happy all the time?' 'Do you know what nirvana looks like?' What they really want to know is if nirvana is possible and achievable, as well as how to get some of it for themselves. They want to know if I have some other worldly secrets for leading a spiritual life.

It might be nice to be completely blissed out all the time; then again it might become tedious and boring. I don't know because my life, like everyone else's, has its ups and downs and twists and turns. Not only do I not have any otherworldly powers or secrets for leading a spiritual life, I am certain that the components of a spiritual life are very much grounded in reality, here and now. This emphasis on truth and reality is not solely a Buddhist thought. Jesus said, 'In order to enter the Kingdom of Heaven, we have to become like little children.' What he meant is that we have to strip away all the accumulated layers of persona and get closer to the open, authentic, loving child that exists in all of us. The great third-century Chinese philosopher Mencius (Mengzi) said, 'The great man is he who does not lose his childlike heart.'

For enlightenment we don't need fancier clothes, or more degrees, or more information. We don't need bigger living spaces, more money, fancier vacations, better jobs, or more influential friends. Enlightenment is everyone's birthright. In order to realize it for ourselves we have to become more grounded, more in touch with who and what we are – what we really are, not what we pretend to be or what society and parents told us to be.

LOOSENING OUR ATTACHMENT
TO PERSONA

Buddhism is all about letting go, and yes, one of the most difficult areas for us to loosen up revolves around image or persona. At the time of the ancient Greeks and Romans, 'persona' was the term applied to the large theatrical masks that actors wore on stage. The two classic masks, of course, are those of joy and sorrow that we've all seen. Actors wore their masks or persona to help audiences tell the good guys from the bad guys and the sad guys from the happy guys.

The Swiss psychiatrist Carl Jung, who helped make the

word 'persona' a common psychological term, said, 'The persona is a compromise between individual and society as to what a man should appear to be.'

According to Jung, the persona is not an accurate reflection of our individuality. Rather it is a mask that we put on in order to fulfill certain societal roles. We wear a persona, like a costume, to help us navigate life's waters. Certainly a well-defined persona can be very helpful in creating the appropriate boundaries that we sometimes need, so using a persona should not always be seen as negative. Sometimes the persona we present is actually connected to the real costumes we wear. When police officers put on their uniforms, they automatically become authority figures. The same thing is true of judges in their robes. When we see medical professionals in hospital garb, they almost by definition take on a certain aura or presence. In fact, when we were children and wore our costumes for play, didn't we assume certain roles, the moment we put them on? Don't we do that, even now, when we put on our party clothes or our exercise gear?

The persona becomes problematic and limiting when it becomes so fixed that it causes us to become frozen in place; the persona becomes problematic when it doesn't allow for growth or authentic feelings – when it insulates us and acts like a shell of armor. Years ago, I knew a very rich woman who lived on the Upper East Side of New York City, on Fifth Avenue. She had enough money to go anywhere she wanted or do anything in the world, but she was so trapped by her role that she never did anything new. Every day she woke up, left her expensive apartment, and travelled twenty blocks by cab to her office. Every night she reversed the process. All of her meals were eaten in one of four or five of the city's best restaurants. She had never been to a coffee shop; she had never been to Chinatown; she had never been to a pizza parlor or bagel joint. She had never walked through the city in which she lived, and all of her shopping was done in one of two stores – Saks or Bloomingdale's – with her personal shopper running interference and even then it was usually her personal shopper who went to the stores. She never let anyone new into her life, and all of her acquaintances were people who were almost exactly like she was in terms of career and socioeconomic status. She was never able to venture out of her role in life. Her persona had taken over.

In a less extreme fashion, this happens to many of us. We become so concerned about projecting the right image that we become afraid to be different or to do anything unusual or 'out of character.' We create armor so thick that nobody can get past it. We're so uneasy around people who look or act differently that we try to avoid them. One of the few times many people are somewhat able to loosen the grip of persona is when they are on vacation. For two weeks out of the year, these men and women suddenly become adventurers. Even though they normally spend every day in constrained environments in business suits, they sign up for wilderness trips or overland bike treks that allow them to loosen the constraints of the personas that they normally project. They don't worry about looking foolish if they act silly or behave in unconventional ways. They come back from their vacations feeling as though this is the only time in the year in which they are truly 'alive.' Doesn't this tell us something about how to feel more alive day to day, throughout the year, and what we might do to bring that about?

There is an old saying that 'travel broadens the mind,' and it does. It helps us get out of the mental prisons of our own making; travel helps us relax and loosen our grip on our limited versions of ourselves. When we go to a different place we are able to revisit who we think we are; we are better able to reinvent who we are. It can be exhilarating to experience, even for a moment, a sense that we could actually be anyone. In foreign cities, for example, we are less reticent about striking up conversations with strangers of all kinds − those who seem completely unlike us in appearance, age, or education and economic background. This is one of the great boons of travel.

DROPPING OUR MASKS AS WE WALK
THE SPIRITUAL PATH

Some people don't easily comprehend how a fixed persona can create a stumbling block on the spiritual path. They don't 'get' how an attachment to a role, a look, or an image can stand in the way of one's inner search. What we need to understand is that the persona we create is tightly wrapped up in the stories we tell ourselves about who we are. In short, the persona is often a veritable gauge of ego clinging. When we take off our armor and discard bits and pieces of the persona, we also let go of ego grasping and clinging. Doing this helps us loosen some of the 'me,' 'my,' and 'mine' thinking that we all indulge in. Many of us, after all, use this kind of thinking as a way of putting up barriers and further solidifying our masks – as in 'my car,' 'my job,' 'my space.' Once again, instead of seeking authentic presence, we seek image, security, and the ego's comfort zone rather than truth and freedom.

This kind of clinging isn't limited to objects. It also extends to our opinions and attitudes; we then use these opinions and attitudes to make us feel superior to others as in:

'I only eat whole grains, tofu, and a few cooked vegetables; anyone who doesn't do the same is courting physical problems.'

'I have very strong views on child rearing; do what I say or you're risking your toddler's emotional well-being.'

'I'm a lifelong Republican/Democrat/Liberal/Conservative/Socialist/Independent; all other points of view are wrong.'

Many people, particularly from my generation, rebelled against the idea of being seen as a 'suit.' They were as harsh in their judgment of people who dressed in a conformist, conservative fashion as the conservatives were of the love beads and long hair that my friends sported in the late Sixties. I know people who practiced a kind of reverse snobbism, avoiding anyone who seemed different than they were. They purposely dressed down, inhabiting the margins of society; they were often proud of how little they needed to get by. For some of them, this continues to be the case. There are people who still refuse to wear suits or ties, no matter where they have been invited. They do this to make a point. Some have even worn tee shirts at the White House. The real point, of course, is that ego is still ego, no matter what it is wearing. Being different can be but another ego trip – an attempt to flaunt an illusion of specialness. Dressing down can be just another kind of conformist dress code. Sometimes just fitting in is the simplest, most unselfish, and humble way to be.

Often these attachments to opinions and our own way of doing things are best recognized by looking at what it is that we judge in others as well as ourselves. Do we, for example, hastily judge others because of their religious or political views? Buddhism teaches that this kind of thinking – no matter what your opinion or point of view – encourages a fixated, dualistic view of the world. When we release and drop our attachment to image, whether that image is represented by appearance, possession, status, role, or attitude, we come closer to our own authentic being – our innate Buddha-nature. We can let go, relax, and simply be ourselves. It is beautiful!

SELF-ACCEPTANCE HELPS US DROP OUR MASKS AND BECOME MORE REAL

In many ways, the personas we construct are simply knee-jerk reactions to our own fears of being judged. Whether the persona we wear is shy and introverted, or exuberant and outgoing, a mask is still a mask. It's a shell, not a meaningful, beating heart. Here's a question we always have to ask: How can we love the world when we haven't learned how to love ourselves? How can we feel loved and accepted if we don't learn to love and accept ourselves?

As we become more and more certain of who we are, we become more grounded and real. We lose our concerns about what others think and are better able to reach out with love and caring. The spiritual path, as both Chogyam Trungpa and Carlos Castaneda's Yaqui Don Juan pointed out, is a warrior's path. It takes bravery to be the shining souls we are meant to be; it takes courage, and even chutzpah, to use our hearts to see beyond the superficial. And yet the heart is like an organ of perception; it could be used to guide and lead us, much like Seeing Eye dogs guide the visually challenged.

There is a Tibetan teaching tale I've always liked. It's about a learned and wise middle-aged lama who receives a visionary visit from a powerful 'dakini,' which is the term Tibetans use to describe sometimes wrathful female goddess-like figures who symbolize truth revealed. In this case, the dakini is Ekajati herself, a formidable, one-eyed, single-breasted protectress of the truth. She comes to issue a prophecy and tells the lama that he should take a consort from a neighboring valley. She says that if he does this, he will be able to discover and unearth hidden teachings that will be of inestimable value to subsequent generations of seekers.

The lama listens to what he is told, and immediately sends three of his monk-disciples to seek the consort that Ekajati has described. While they are gone, the lama keeps vigil in his shrine room, praying and meditating.

After a week, the monks return. But they are alone. 'Where

is the prophesied consort I am waiting for?' the lama asks.

'We found no one suitable for you,' the monks tell him. 'The only woman we saw was a ragged woodcutter, blind in one eye, wearing tattered clothes, carrying a rusty old sickle, with some gnarled branches of firewood on her bent back. She was a truly terrifying woman. Certainly not the type who would seem to be a suitable consort for someone of your sacred stature.'

'That must be her,' the lama says, jumping up in delight. 'That harpy is none other than the great Dharma protectress Ekajati in human disguise. Please immediately go find her and bring her here!'

The surprised and chagrined disciples are compelled to rush right back out and hunt high and low until they eventually find the woman, who appears to be as wild and crooked as the firewood she carries on her back. When the head lama sees her, he greets her with open arms and bows with an open heart that is filled with respect and delight; unlike his students, he recognized the authentic nature of the woman before him and knows a true dakini when he sees one.

The master delights in finding this woman to be his true soul mate and consort; the awesome lady in turn regally rules his household and inspires everyone who dares to enter her intense presence. As promised, the lama finds numerous spiritual treasures, revelations, and teachings which he shares with Dharma seekers. This lineage of rediscovered ancient teaching treasures remains with us today.

The point of this story, of course, is that the lama was able to see his own spiritual muse and consort for who she is only because he was supremely confident in his own judgment and sense of his own mission and purpose in life. He didn't care what others thought. In his search for authentic truth, he had no time for the superficial. He was immune to the deception of appearances.

When we are able to let go and abandon the extraneous, we are left with bare essence – the authentic Buddha-nature within. Your inner Buddha is sublimely confident and sure; he/she is at home with everyone, everywhere. When we are in touch with our inner Buddhas, we no longer need to eat in restaurants where we can see and be seen by the 'people who count,' whoever those people might be. We don't need to avoid people who don't share our worldview. We don't worry about being liked or fitting in; we can follow our own path, our own dancing star. When we are in touch with our inner Buddhas, we are fearlessly able to accept others because we accept ourselves, for who and what we are. We have arrived home, at home and at one with ourselves. This is the journey's goal.

YOU CAN'T IMITATE AUTHENTIC PRESENCE

Sometimes we meet those who have a genuine sense of authentic presence. Often these individuals are powerful spiritual leaders or charismatic teachers with awe-inspiring energy. What sometimes happens to the students of such teachers is that they attempt to mimic the master's behavior. There is a

Japanese Zen story about a master of old who had a unique way of teaching. This master is very well known because he answers all questions that are put to him by simply holding up one inscrutable forefinger. A young monk in the zendo (meditation hall) is very impressed by this, so impressed that he decides to imitate the master. The next time someone asks the acolyte a question, he holds up one finger. He does this again and again. It works for the master, why shouldn't it work for him?

The venerable Zen master hears of this, and after a while he calls the boy to him. 'Tell me,' the master asks, 'who is the true Buddha?' The young monk holds up his one imitating finger. In one swift move, the master reaches out and cuts off the monk's finger with a sword. The young monk is stunned; he screams — a high, primal scream that is authentically his own. As the monk's sounds pierce the quiet of the zendo, the master holds up his one finger, and at that moment, the young monk is instantly enlightened. The moral of this strange little story, of course, is that you can't get real through imitation. By taking away the imitation, the false pointer-finger, the boy returned to his real Buddha.

Just as we all have Buddha-nature, we all have unique authentic presence. Everything about each and every one of us is different. From our fingerprints to our voice prints, each of us is authentic in his or her own way. This authenticity is something to be nurtured, cherished, and celebrated. It is probably our greatest gift, a treasure we can rediscover within ourselves, in the midst of the gritty details of our very own life.

Some people, of course, are so authentic and real that the very air around them seems to reverberate with their presence. There is a story that's told in Asia about a celebrated martial arts master of ancient China. The master was absolutely indomitable. When he was in combat he moved like a whirlwind; no one could touch him, and he seemed impervious to fear, pain, illness, or any form of attack. When he was fighting, this master would bellow *'Yaaaarghhh!!!!!!!!!!!!!!!!!!'* – loud enough to shake the firmament.

This forceful master taught his students to face life and death with equanimity, no matter what – whether surrounded by hundreds of brigands or by a vision of hundreds of Buddhas. One night, the master was walking up in the mountains by himself, and he was attacked by a dozen or more sword-carrying robbers. He fought intensely, and managed to ward most of them off, but he was one man, and they outnumbered him twelve to one. Finally just before dawn, one of them ran a sword through his stomach, and the master shouted *'Yaaaarghh!!!!!!!!!!!!!!'* All who heard it, far and wide, knew it was his death cry. It was so loud that the entire slumbering countryside was awakened and enlightened by the shout. Such was this master's connection to reality.

CHOOSING TO BE AUTHENTIC –
A SPIRITUAL PRACTICE

When I was growing up, many of the families in my neighborhood covered their living room furniture in plastic to protect it. I hated sitting on those slippery plastic covers. They seemed false, as well as uncomfortable. Now I know a lot of people who work in large metal and glass buildings with windows that never open. More than a few of them complain that many things in their work environment are false, including the air, which they say is so totally unnatural and stale that it sometimes makes people sick. These days it seems as though we are all somehow affected by places and situations that lack authenticity. It's a real spiritual challenge not to take on the plastic trappings of our surroundings.

There are so many times in life when we feel as though we have to pretend to be something we're not; there are so many times when we know that the people around us are pretending too. It's wearisome, isn't it? We pretend everything is fine, even when it isn't; we pretend to be brave and strong when we are frightened and vulnerable; we pretend to be happy when we're sad; we pretend to know what we're doing when we are totally confused; we pretend to know what we're talking about when we're merely voicing words. We do it so often that pretense and inauthenticity can become habits, till we are as if lost amidst all the spin and smoke and mirrors, and have lost touch with our essential selves and the fundamental reality of our own lives.

How many hours each day do we spend feeling disconnected, alienated, or as though we are playing a role? Some people complain that they feel as though they are always playing the role of sycophant – 'sucking up' to people they don't want to be with. Others say their lives seem consumed with titles, achievements, and 'resumes' – theirs as well as everybody else's. Many feel oppressed by the burden of constantly trying to be what others want them to be. Still others complain that some days they feel uncomfortable in their own skin. Where does this all leave us? Doesn't it ultimately make us feel as though we are eating too much junk food?

Who do we think we are fooling in the long run? Who's watching? In the crucial moments of life and death – moments of crisis, joy, and tragedy – there is no room to pretend. We are forced to be real. Maybe that's why these are some of our most memorable moments. Why does it take tragedy or crisis to force us to be on the spot, to be authentically present, to be just who we are. James Joyce wrote about one of his characters, 'Mr Bloom lived a short distance from his body.' Don't we all? But that's not a terminal condition. We can reconnect and be ourselves, the genuine article, the real McCoy.

Reconnecting to Your Own Truth

One of the ways we can begin to cultivate a more authentic presence is by giving ourselves some time in which we make a commitment to be as true, honest, and real as we can possibly be. Set aside some time – it could be an hour a day, one day a week, or even one day a month. During this time, try to keep everything you do, say, and think as centered, real, and genuinely grounded in your actual moment-to-moment daily experience as possible. Be the right person in the right place at the right time by being at one with any given moment, just as it presents itself. Here are some suggestions on how to do this:

1. BE NATURAL.

Where do you feel most comfortable and natural? Think about the places and activities that make you feel most grounded. Think about the people who make you feel as though you can be yourself. Do you feel most comfortable when you're home wearing flannel pajamas and eating comfort food? Comfort and naturalness encourage healing. Naturalness is the opposite of anxiety and stress, so let the real you emerge. Don't put on airs or try to impress anyone. Hang loose and do what comes naturally. Give rein to your innate creativity; let your wholesome natural impulses guide you. Feel free and unencumbered enough – unselfconscious enough – to just be you. I think you'll love it.

2. BE SIMPLE.

As you interrelate with the world, try to keep your language and your dealings with others as simple and straightforward as possible. Keep your dealings with yourself as simple as possible as well. Don't get involved in long convoluted conversations or interior monologues. Have a simple meal; take a simple walk; perform a simple chore without hurrying; sit on a chair and look at the trees and sky. When you speak, take care to be absolutely truthful. Try not to add anything unnecessary or extraneous to your life. Instead, in the immortal words of Thoreau, 'simplify, simplify, simplify.'

3. LOOSEN YOUR TENDENCY TO CONTROL.

As you do inner work and become more authentic, try to let go of some of your anxieties and tendency to control situations and others. Resist the impulse to interfere unnecessarily with outcomes. Don't struggle unduly to make things happen the way you want them to. Just rest and enjoy the moment. Let others be. Let yourself be as well. Let it be.

4. BE AUTHENTIC.

Put all your stories about yourself and others aside. Instead try to become like a child and experience everything as though it were brand-new. Ask yourself, 'What do I really feel?' 'What do I really want?' 'What is this?' Don't be unduly influenced by external values and conditions. Be honest and straightforward with yourself and others. Live moment to moment, as an intentional exercise in consciousness raising and centeredness.

5. STAY OPEN TO THE WORLD AROUND YOU.

Be inclusive and accepting. Try not to be judgmental and critical. Lose some of your armor; invite and allow others to share your experience. Be open to the sights, smells, and sounds in your immediate environment. Enjoy and appreciate reality as it unfolds. Edit and control less; appreciate more; and savor the qualities of whatever comes your way.

6. STAY AWARE.

Pay attention and be mindful of your experience moment by moment. Just relax and let yourself be. See with your inner eye; hear with your inner ear. Don't let superficial judgments get in the way of reality. Attend to the present. This is the holy now; don't overlook it.

7. STAY WISE.

Practice nonattachment and letting go of the extraneous. Let go of old judgments and attitudes. Let go of old hurts and angers. Let go of old prejudices, biases, and preconceptions. Cultivate a fresh, penetrating, vividly wakeful and acute sense of discernment and discrimination. See if you can really think for yourself and directly apprehend things just as they are.

8. BE SPONTANEOUS AND LET YOUR ENERGY FLOW NATURALLY.

Spontaneity is natural and authentic. Don't be inhibited about expressing positive energy. Sing in the shower or chant on the street if that's what you feel like doing. Don't be afraid to dance, play, or just be silly. Let your energy expand and sweep you up. Spread your arms and whirl like a dervish. Fling your hands up to the sky and shout, *'AAAAAAAhhh!* Yes!' (Why not?)

CHAPTER FIVE

Letting Go, Getting Real

What a relief it was for me to go to my first meditation retreat and hear people speak the truth so clearly – the First Noble Truth that life is difficult and painful, just by its very nature, not because we're doing it wrong. I was so relieved to meet people who were willing to say life is difficult, often painful, and who still looked fine about admitting it. Most important, they looked *happy*. This was tremendously reassuring to me. I thought to myself, 'Here are people who are just like me, who have lives just like mine, who know the truth and are willing to name it and are all right with it.'

– Sylvia Boorstein

The Buddha taught that this is an imperfect world; nothing is totally the way we want it to be. That's reality. By the time we become teenagers most of us have discovered that nowhere is this reality more blatant than in our interactions with others. Let's admit it: Relationships, by their very nature, are challenging.

People don't always behave the way we want them to; they don't say what we want them to say; they don't do what we want them to do; they don't treat us the way we want to be treated. But what can we do about this painful fact? What are our options and choices? After all, few of us want to retreat from the world. We know that human connection is essential to our happiness and crucial for our personal growth and well-being.

Perhaps one of the reasons spiritual masters have an easier time dealing with others is that they realize that everything, even our closest friendships, will be at least a little bit flawed, a little bit imperfect. This is the nature of life. That certainly doesn't mean that we should give up on the possibility of true friendship or intimacy. It does mean that we can find more skillful, grounded, balanced, and mindful ways of relating to each other and the world. Spiritual intelligence consistently reminds us to view personal relationships with the wisdom that allows us to appreciate their ups and downs as being part of our spiritual path and inner growth.

Our spiritual intentions and aspirations for enlightenment are abundantly clear: We are striving to become more caring and patient, more loving and generous, more wholesome, open, and wise. We can't easily cultivate these qualities in a vacuum; this practice requires interactions with others. Our relationships, whether they be fleeting or long term, casual or intense, provide personal laboratories in which we can put our spiritual intentions into practice. In fact, finding ways to skillfully and compassionately interact with others is a large part of what the spiritual path is all about.

Incorporating our spiritual aspirations into our daily inter-actions with others is no easy challenge. A friend of mine, Diane, recently had her car stolen. She reacted with impres-sive equanimity, telling herself that in the greater scheme of things losing a car is not such a big deal. Friends helped by driving Diane places, she rediscovered the joys of walking to the store, and she no longer faced the struggle of alternate side of the street parking. She stayed patient as she spent hours on the phone; she stayed calm as she spent days collecting paper-work and filling out forms for the police and the insurance company. She even cultivated thoughts of loving-kindness toward the thief! But then it turned out that there was a glitch in her automobile title; before the insurance company could make payment on her loss she needed to go to the Department of Motor Vehicles, known affectionately as the DMV, and get duplicates of some missing paperwork.

Diane dutifully arrived at the DMV at 10:00 A.M. The line snaked out to the door. Two and a half hours later she had been back and forth, going from one line to another, more than a half dozen times. She had filled out many confusing forms, some of them in error, and she was still trying to find someone who could resolve her problem. But none of the DMV employees she spoke to seemed able to help. At first Diane was quiet, patient, and polite, but finally she lost it. Her equanimity visa expired. She went 'postal' at the DMV; she didn't actually kick a wastebasket, but she thought of it. Diane was not alone in her exasperation. She was surrounded by dozens of other grim-faced motorists. People were moaning and groaning; people were arguing and complaining. *Surely,* she thought, *this would test the patience of even the most committed saint or stoic Zen practitioner.* Diane wanted to stay calm and balanced, but in the stress of the moment she found herself 'separating' from her intentions.

Even the most experienced meditation practitioners sometimes forget that meditation training is intended as a practice that will help us deal with others, as well as life's ups and downs, more skillfully. We see the truth of this when we observe the great meditation masters; they can remain unperturbable — as well as aware — no matter what is going on around them. It's as though they carry their own atmosphere with them wherever they go, maintaining equanimity independent of all circumstances. This is one of the many benefits of meditation. It helps us relate to life and people in a more balanced way.

When I was growing up, everyone told me how impatient and overactive I was. I loved sports, and my whole life seemed to be about quick reaction time; I always had to set my own pace, which was fast, and do things my own way. I had little tolerance for what I perceived to be a waste of time. Somehow, thirty years later, it's come about that people tell me how calm and patient I am. I have a friend who says that she both loves and hates driving when I am in her passenger seat. She loves it because I'm so calm; she hates it because I'm so damned calm. She calls me preternaturally calm, and says that it sometimes makes her even more anxious and reactive. So occasionally if we are together in her car, I act a little jumpy and reactive. It's our little joke. It usually takes her a few minutes to figure out what I'm doing, and then she gets mad at me. Then I say, 'Caught you,' and we both have a good laugh, which relaxes her.

USING MEDITATIVE TECHNIQUES AS RELATIONSHIP TOOLS

Leave the body at rest, like an unmovable mountain.
Leave the speech at rest, like an unstrung guitar.
Leave the mind at rest, like a shepherd after dusk who has brought his flock home and sits content by the warm fire.
— Tibetan Meditation instruction

TRADITIONAL MEDITATION INSTRUCTION

Stop what you are doing; stop what you are thinking.

Get comfortable. Relax.

Find your balance. If you are sitting cross-legged on a floor, settle your legs so they feel as though they are where they belong. If you are using a cushion, adjust it the way you like it. If you are sitting on a chair, place your feet evenly on the floor. If you are standing, let your body settle.

Keep your spine straight and your body relaxed. Let your shoulders drop.

Settle into the present moment.

Let your energy settle naturally; let your breath settle naturally; let your thoughts settle naturally.

Collect yourself.

Come home to the present moment.

Arrive where you are meant to be.

Sit in the present moment.

Breathe in, breathe out.

As you inhale, focus on the in breath. Count one.

As you exhale, focus on the out breath. Count two.

One on the inhalation, two on the exhalation.

Ride the breath.

Surf the breath.

Rest your mind on the simple, regular, calming wave of breathing.

Become aware of what you are feeling. Notice the physical sensations that your body is experiencing. Notice the sensation in your shoulders, notice the thoughts that bubble up to the surface of your mind. Notice them and simply let them go. No need to work them out or get caught up in them. Continue breathing. Focus on the in breath. Focus on the out breath. And let go.

Settle in the present moment. Stay aware of actual perceived moment-to-moment happenings: a slight pain in your shoulder, the low roar of an airplane climbing in the sky, the sound of the wind rustling through the trees, the muted voices from a neighbor's TV coming through the wall, the hissing of a radiator. Don't suppress your perceptions, feelings, or awareness; simply notice what is happening and then let it dissolve as the new moment begins. Stay awake; remain alert; pay attention.

Breathe in. . . . Breathe out. Stay focused. Let go of each breath, don't hang on. Let go of each thought; don't hang on. Note your thoughts; notice them, and let them go. If your shoulder hurts, name it 'discomfort,' and let it go. If the airplane noise breaks your concentration, name it 'hearing, hearing,' and let it go. If the temperature in the room gets chilly, name it 'cold,' and let it go. Let go of your worries; don't hang on. Let go of any attempts to control your mind; don't hang on. With each exhalation, let go a little more.

This is meditation.

As meditators, we train ourselves in meditative awareness. This is called mindfulness. Let's say, for example, that while I am meditating, I feel an itch in my big toe. I am aware of the feeling in the present moment, but I let go of any tendency to react at that moment. It's enough to be aware of the itchy toe. I don't have to do anything about it. I can just let it go . . . Be aware of it, and let it be. This is the meaning of letting go.

Lama Anagarika Govinda, author of *Foundations of Tibetan Mysticism,* was a German-born Westerner who travelled to Asia to study with Buddhist masters back in the 1920s. He defined meditation as follows: 'Meditation is the way to reconnect the individual with the whole, to make us aware of our continuing connection and communion, which has never really been broken off.'

Meditation trains us to return to simplicity by being aware of the essentials and letting go of the extraneous. This is an invaluable skill for our complex, busy lives, where each of us has a lot we could learn to let go of. I'm not talking only about our worldly possessions; I'm talking about attitudes, behavioral quirks, habits, resentments about the past, as well as fanciful dreams about the future. Meditation helps us let go of our knee-jerk reactions and responses to people as well as situations; it trains us to let go of our attachment to discursive thinking and ego identification, which makes us perceive everything as being connected to 'me' or 'mine.' We can apply these lessons to everything we do.

Let's say your weary and cranky spouse greets you at the door tonight complaining that you neglected to do your share of the household chores. Your immediate reaction may be defensive; you may feel angry and misunderstood. Here's where meditation techniques pay off. The principles of meditative awareness, properly applied, give you the tools to notice and be aware of 'anger' without acting on it. You can have the feeling, but that feeling doesn't mean that you are compelled to lash out. You can choose to just notice the anger without judging whether it is good or bad. It simply is. This is what is known as 'choiceless awareness.' It means you are able to be aware of what is happening without necessarily making judgments or having preferences. You don't have to react. This gives you the time to consider the bigger picture. It gives you the time to remember your highest intentions and purpose; it gives you the space you need to be able to intentionally decide and choose how to act. In these few seconds, you might have a completely different and more compassionate thought, such as 'My poor spouse must be really tired.' If you respond to your spouse with empathy, caring, and compassionate concern instead of annoyance, you will be creating better, more positive karma – and a better relationship.

In Buddhist practice we learn first to meditate silently – frequently, in a room alone; or with others who are sharing the same activity. In silent meditation, it's relatively easy to recognize and be aware of the thoughts, emotions, and conditioning that intrude and interfere with our concentration. Then when we have mastered that, we take the lessons of meditation out into the world where all of our buttons, our samskaras, are likely to be pushed regularly.

These days, we are often told that faster is better, but when it comes to emotional reaction time, slower is often the wiser way to go. Meditation helps us extend our reaction time. In this way, we are given another second or two more before we respond. For example, this morning Frank walked into his office to discover that his boss, Freya, was furious at him. It seems that the computer was acting up yet again, and Freya's frustrations made her irrationally blame Frank. A few years ago Frank might have been very upset by the unfairness of Freya's anger; all of his buttons would have been pushed, and he would have been thrown into a tailspin of strong feelings that would have made him react immediately. Now, after several years of meditating, he doesn't feel compelled to respond. Instead he has control over his responses. He can take his time and make a conscious decision about what he wants to say and how, when, and where he wants to say it. Frank is aware enough to assess the situation; he knows he doesn't *have* to react. Maybe he should let Freya rant; maybe he should quit; maybe he should just sigh, breathe, and relax. Frank has choices, and he has mastery over his reactions. He is thus able to be the master of himself.

Having said that, I think it's important that we don't put too much pressure on ourselves. Reaching this level of awareness is a process. We shouldn't be too impatient or idealistic about how 'perfectly' restrained and even-minded we should be. When we get embroiled in situations in which we are heavily vested, it's difficult not to react impulsively. Therefore I think it's a good idea to approach ourselves, as well as others, with compassion, patience, sensitivity, and gentleness.

I am always trying to adopt a more meditative, conscious approach to interpersonal dealings. I have learned that I have to be careful not to think of it as a quick fix prescription. We can't approach relationships with absolute dictums such as, 'I won't say anything; I'll just bite my lip.' This kind of absolute doesn't work very well. It's a little like unrealistic New Year's resolutions that are just asking to be broken and unfulfilled. It's much better to simply try to cultivate some kind of mindful self-awareness that will help keep us in touch and up-to-date with our inner selves and state of being, moment to moment.

Simply watch yourself. Be aware. Notice how you react with others. Try to bring microscopic clarity of attention to all your interactions, and try to perceive which of your buttons is being pushed. Notice the habitual, reflexive, and often unconscious reactions arising. Name them, and let them go. See if by so doing, you can create a more spacious and open approach to your relationships. See if you can become more skillful, intelligent, and even-handed. Doing this doesn't mean that you will never again get angry or resentful; it does mean that you can channel emotions like anger and resentment more effectively. It's okay, for example, to get angry, realizing that there are several steps between anger arising inside and anger becoming external aggression. Emotions like anger are just emotional energy. We can choose to intervene between the experience of anger and the acting out.

I like to advise people to follow a little four-step mindfulness practice as a way of handling their emotions.

1. NOTICE WHAT YOU ARE FEELING.

Don't deny or bury what you are feeling. Simply notice each feeling that arises and call it by its name – anger, pride, jealousy, covetousness, lustful desire, irritation, or annoyance, for example.

2. RATHER THAN REJECTING IT, CRADLE THE FEELING WITH LOVE AND MINDFULNESS; EMBRACE IT WITH AWARENESS.

Recognize the feeling for what it is – simply a feeling that is arising. Don't get angry at yourself or the feeling, but don't let it take over and carry you away.

3. USE DISCRIMINATING AWARENESS TO REFLECT ON WHAT YOU ARE FEELING.

Analyze and examine the feeling. Are you having a knee-jerk reaction? Is your feeling justified? (Perhaps it is a reasonable response.)

4. BEHAVE IN AN INTENTIONAL AND WISE MANNER.

Make a wise decision about how to react to what you are feeling at the moment. Remember that no matter how strong your feeling is, nothing remains the same. The feeling will change, and another will take its place. With that in mind, take the long view; use spiritual intelligence and an understanding of karma to make an appropriate choice about how to act.

When we handle our feelings mindfully in this way, we become more emotionally stable, trustworthy, and reliable. Through the power of insight, our responses become more balanced and more in line with what is really happening.

BECOME THE REAL YOU, THE PERSON YOU WERE MEANT TO BE

Meditation practice specifically cultivates moment-to-moment mindfulness. When we are mindful, we are significantly less likely to be reflexively reacting to all the emotional buttons, or samskaras, that were implanted in us by past events or behavior. None of us wants to go through life mindlessly responding out of old conditionings and twisted prejudices from the past. We've all, for example, had the experience of mindlessly saying things that we heard our parents say; this is one of the ways that prejudice and intolerance get passed on. Mindfulness helps us relate to others in ways that allow us to be more true to who we really want to be; it helps us be more authentic, which, in turn, helps us ground our relationships in present reality and current time. It is time we caught up with ourselves in this way.

Bringing this level of awareness into our dealings with others is not about pretending or manipulating or trying to be dishonest with our feelings and emotions. We are simply trying to become more mindful, compassionate, and virtuous – more Buddha-like in everything we do.

The basic essential premise of Buddhism is this: Each of us, at core, is a Buddha. We are all Buddhas. Innately, each of us has the compassion and love of a Buddha; each of us has the virtue and morality of a Buddha; each of us has the patience, acceptance, and tolerance of a Buddha; each of us has the spiritual energy and endurance of a Buddha; each of us has the concentration and meditative powers of a Buddha; each of us has within us the wisdom of a potential Buddha. It is latent within us. We only have to unfold our spiritual treasure from within ourselves.

Meditation is a technique that we use to help us return to our essential, original nature – our Buddha-nature. We are training ourselves in how to respond to everything in life from that basic core of essential goodness. We are training ourselves to relinquish the illusions, fantasies, and distractions that confuse our lives; we are learning to 'let go' of the conditioned responses and habits that keep us stuck. The practice of meditation is a tool that helps us cast off the barnacles of conditioning and find the beautiful, wise, and loving Buddha buried under all the sludge. *This is the real you.*

If you want to know how to react and what to do in each situation in life, ask yourself how Buddha would react – what would Buddha do? If you want to know what to do in life, ask yourself what Wisdom and Love would do in such a situation.

When we start with this base, with this intention, we begin to create a blueprint, a template for how to relate to others. Life is difficult, it's true. It's up to us to try to make it easier and happier – for others and for ourselves as well so that all may have what they need and aspire to. These are the intentions of a Buddha.

LETTING GO OF EXPECTATIONS OF 'PERFECTION'

Last year I took my wonderful dog, Chandi, in for grooming just before Christmas. When the grooming was finished, she looked as fluffy as a white angora rabbit. The groomer had even tied a sweet little red and green bow on her collar. After we returned home from the groomer, I made the mistake of letting her go out unattended in the fields around my house. Within minutes she had discovered the smelliest, dirtiest clump of 'something' she could find, and she rolled around – and around – in it. By the time she was finished even her red bow was wet and filthy. There went my image of my perfect, beautiful dog.

It's never easy to face the fact that nothing is perfect. Don't we rail against our significant others when they reveal flaws we would rather not see? The Buddha reminded us time and again that everything is flawed. That's reality. Reality means taking off the tinted glasses we are wearing – whether those glasses are tinted with a rosy or dark hue. Meditation helps us train ourselves in clear seeing, in looking at the world without distortion, directly and objectively. As spiritual seekers, we are committed to cultivating clear seeing, clear hearing, and clear thinking – in short, clear perception. This leads to wisdom and truth.

This is an interesting approach to apply to our interactions with others since nowhere are we more likely to be guided by fantasies and unrealistic expectations than in the arena of interpersonal relationships. Don't we all cling to our fantasies about how things and others should be? We get angry at our parents because they are not always perfect; we get angry at our children because they are not always perfect; we get angry at our mates because they are not always perfect. Who doesn't cling to the 'soul mate' fantasy, in which our significant other is the one person who is always able to relate to us with perfect understanding and acceptance – a charming prince or princess who can be like a savior to us.

Seekers often have a tendency to overidealize and can therefore be particularly prone to unrealistic expectations. We can, for example, be so deeply attached to our fantasies and our Prince and Princess Charming dreams that we undermine all our relationships with demands based on expectations that cannot possibly be fulfilled. We are often so filled with fantasies about what should be that we fail to acknowledge or appreciate what is. Approaching life with expectations is an invitation to frustration. However, with no expectations, we experience no disappointment.

Marge and Patti are two women married to men with similar personality quirks. Marge's husband Dan doesn't like parties and refuses to accompany her to most social events;

Patti's husband John feels the same way Dan does. That's where the similarities end. Marge believes that husbands and wives should only socialize together and says she feels strange going out without her husband; on those nights when they are invited somewhere she stays home with Dan and complains about it. Patti, on the other hand, kisses John good-bye, goes out, has a nice time with her friends, and returns home a few hours later to have a bedtime snack and chat with her husband. Marge and Patti are dealing with similar issues in such different ways that it changes the entire dynamic of their relationships. Faced with the same situation, one has made a workable, satisfying choice while one has chosen not to make it work.

Buddhist teachings consistently remind us that everything is relative. Not long ago I was at a New Year's Eve gathering in the Boston area. At midnight, it was 45 degrees outdoors, and we were all commenting on how warm it was. If it had been 45 degrees on a night in July, we would all be complaining about the cold. This exemplifies how our concepts and expectations alter our experience of everything, even the temperature.

This simply points out another way in which we become attached to our views, opinions, and ideas about everything, including 'how life should be.' The Vietnamese teacher Thich Nhat Hanh wrote, 'Attachment to views is the greatest impediment to the spiritual path.'

Some of the most common misinterpretations people make about Buddhism involve the ideal of nonattachment; they often assume that being Buddhist means giving up those they love. In *The Mind and the Way,* the Theravadin Buddhist teacher Ajahn Sumedho writes:

'If you're coming from a high-minded position in which you think you shouldn't be attached to anything, then you come up with ideas like, 'Well I can't be Buddhist because I love my wife . . .' Those kinds of thoughts come from the view that you shouldn't be attached. The recognition of attachment doesn't mean that you get rid of your wife. It means that you free yourself from wrong views about yourself and your wife. Then you find that there's love there, but it's not attached. It's not distorting, clinging, and grasping. The empty mind is quite capable of caring about others and loving in the pure sense of love. But any attachment will always distort that. If you love someone and then start grasping, things get complicated; then what you love causes you pain. For example, you love your children, but if you become attached to them . . . you have all kinds of ideas about what they should be and what you want them to be . . . as we let go of attachment, we find that our natural way of relating is to love. We find that we are able to allow our children to be as they are, rather than having fixed ideas of what we want them to be.'

The Tibetan Book of the Dead reminds us that we create our own phantasmagoria; the specters that loom large on our horizon are put there mainly by our own minds. Our attitudes, opinions, and expectations are overlaid upon reality; they shape our world and get in our way. Nothing is perfect, but then again nothing is all bad either. There is an ancient Zen poem known as 'Trust in the Heart Sutra'; it was written in China by the Third Zen Patriarch. One of my favorite lines from it is:

> *'Do not seek for truth,*
> *Merely cease to cherish your own ideas and opinions.'*

A Buddhist sutra says, 'Things are not what they seem to be, nor are they otherwise.' This reminds us not to be so invested in what we think and expect. Better to remain open to life and what it brings. Be open to the moment. When we have no expectations, there are no disappointments. If we make an appointment and the person we hope to meet doesn't show up, we wouldn't be disappointed if we didn't have a certain expectation. The Buddhist lesson is that everything that is put together eventually falls apart. That doesn't mean that reality is shattered. Reality is what it is, forever free and untouched by our projections and interpretations, as well as our hopes and anxieties about it. In short, there is a certain amount of joy to be found even in a muddy dog. It's still the same lovable dog, after all, no matter how dirty she gets! I must remember that.

KEEPING OUR CONNECTIONS
AUTHENTIC AND HONEST

The best relationships we have are genuine and real. In real relationships we don't have to pretend; we aren't afraid of knowing our partners, nor are we afraid to be known. Real relationships are strengthened by authenticity and truth telling. We know this intellectually, but nonetheless in actual day-to-day relating, it's all too easy to slip back into habitual patterns that are primarily defensive and self-serving.

A large part of any Buddhist contemplative practice revolves around mindfulness. We try to stay in the present moment, in the now, and we observe ourselves mindfully. Watching ourselves, we become aware of unnecessary and self-defeating attitudes; watching ourselves we learn to let go of inauthentic behavior that keeps us stuck in the ruts of our lives. Here's a short list of some of the most common behaviors that we all need to recognize:

✳ CONTROLLING BEHAVIOR

When we're trying to control others, what we are typically doing is 'watching' somebody else instead of being mindful of our own actions. Whenever we find ourselves expending energy trying to change or control somebody else, the antidote is breathing in and out mindfully and letting go of the impulse.

✳ HIDDEN AGENDAS

We've all met people who seem to approach the world almost as though they have battle plans – deeply secret agendas which only they know. To some small degree we probably all indulge in this kind of behavior. How much better and less exhausting it is to be honest and forthcoming.

✳ SUPERFICIAL VALUES

How can we be honest with our friends if our basic responses to others are being formed by superficial values? Since we occupy a world in which many try to resolve their problems by going shopping, it's easy to understand why this kind of thinking is so prevalent. Just remember: Superficial values cloud our vision; they keep us from seeing the light in our fellow beings.

✳ GOSSIP AND TALE TELLING

Have you ever been hypocritical or 'two-faced' with a friend? Have you ever gossiped about somebody until that person entered the room, and then became extremely friendly and amiable? The essence of morality and virtue is represented by the wisdom of not harming others, even with words.

✳ EXPLOITATION

We all want to be in I-thou relationships that are open, respectful, and honest; nobody wants to be seen as an object. Who wants to be manipulated or used for someone else's gain? Not me and not you! Exploitation is not the true purpose of our being here together on this good earth. If and when we can connect with others, recognizing them as not much different from ourselves in terms of needs and desires, then who can we exploit, who can we objectify, and who can we deceive?

✳ DEPENDENT CLINGING

Buddhism makes a distinction between love and clinging. I think this needs repeating time and again. We need to be mindful, no matter how much we may care about specific people, that it's wise to recognize the differences between love and clinging, compassion and demanding neediness. Buddhism reminds us to cultivate balance and equanimity. In this way, our relationships are based more on openness and a free-flowing give-and-take instead of being like Velcro or sticky fly paper. When love becomes overly laced with clinging, it can go awry; we become needy and co-dependent. Jealousy is an example of love gone awry.

✳ LIVING IN THE PAST

We all carry our own ghosts, and too often, we find ourselves relating to the people in our lives as though they are specters from the past. If we quarreled with our parents, we continue the same patterns with our mates; if we were jealous of our siblings, we run the risk of dealing with everyone with an undercurrent of sibling rivalry. It's almost impossible to have authentic, meaningful, heart-to-heart, soul-to-soul relationships until we learn to loosen the subconscious hold that our ghosts have on us. Psychotherapy and introspection can help us be able to do so.

Mindfulness is always the perfect reminder to let go of convoluted logic and tangled, self-defeating behavior. The practice of mindfulness helps us be more present and deal with situations as they occur. It helps us be attentive and let go of the past. It helps us see reality, and it helps us be more authentically true to ourselves.

BREATHE, SMILE, LET GO

Breathe In . . . Count One.
Breathe Out . . . Count Two.
Breathe In . . . Count One.
Breathe Out . . . Count Two.
Breathe In . . . Count One.
Breathe Out . . . Count Two.
Smile.
Relax.
You are fully present. Enjoy the miracle
of the present moment.
Peace and joy.

AUTHENTIC LISTENING

We bring greater spirituality as well as authenticity to our relationships by genuinely listening to the sounds and voices of the world. Start listening, and see what happens. Few among us can truly hear what others are saying. Instead we hear what we want to hear. I once saw a very funny cartoon of a dog listening to a person speaking. The dog was blotting out all the words except those that related to food. Blah, blah, blah, dinner . . . Blah, blah, blah, steak. In some ways we all do the same thing. When I was in college, I was working on a project for which I was tape recording some interviews. I would listen to the person who was being interviewed, and I would think that I had a clear idea about what was being said. Then later I would read the actual typed transcript of the interview, and I would inevitably be surprised by how little I had truly heard. Too often I discovered that I had related primarily to the things that interested me, and just like the cartoon pooch, failed to pay attention to those words that didn't automatically capture my attention.

I noticed the same thing in monastic retreat. A group of monks and nuns would gather every afternoon after lunch for intensive two- to three-hour teachings from one of our learned Tibetan lamas. Afterward, when I compared my notes with those of the others, I would sometimes discover that it was almost as though we had been listening to different teachings. This was true even of those who, like myself, had been scribbling intently, trying to write down almost every word that our teacher said. The fact is that we had all emphasized slightly different points; our interpretations of what we had heard and what were the main points were simply not the same.

True listening accurately reflects whatever appears, just like a mirror, without error or distortion. Discriminating, mirror-like wisdom can discern subtle nuances and distinctions and can recognize deeper connections, patterns, and implications.

The oral Sufi tradition says that 'Mohammed is an ear.' This puts an interesting spin on the role of the prophet. Mohammed is seen not only as a speaker, but as someone who is attuned to listening to the 'sacred other.' We also can listen and hear the sacred other, whether that other is God, mate, colleague, or child.

One of the biggest complaints that people have about their relationships is that the other is not listening; consequently they don't feel heard. It can be an act of generosity to give people an ear, which is a spiritual practice – good for us, and good for others. It doesn't mean that we can fix them or fix others, but we are helping just by giving them a hearing, by providing a sounding board. We all need it, and we are capable of doing it. It's reciprocal, like breathing in and breathing out.

LISTENING WITH THE THIRD EAR

In Buddhist centers and retreats around the world, meditation sessions often begin with the sound of a gong. At the Japanese Zen Temple in Bodh Gaya, there is a large brass gong, the size of a truck tire. Hanging next to it is a huge tree trunk–sized log. At sunset each evening two monks come out and together swing the log, striking it against the gong. I can still recall the reverberating sound, across all the years. In Tibet, practitioners are often called to meditation by gongs of different sizes; sometimes Tibetan singing bells are used for this purpose or long horns that fill an entire valley with the resonant sound.

Whenever I meditate, I slowly strike my bronze, bowl-shaped Japanese singing gong with a wooden mallet. I do this three times, letting it reverberate as long as possible. This is how I begin and end each session. When we enjoy these beautiful sounds, we may think we are ringing these instruments for our own ears, but Tibetans say we are also offering music up to the ears of all the Buddhas – including our own inner Buddhas. If we are able to hear the sounds, the little Buddha within will begin stirring. Sometimes we use large drums that resonate in our hearts and stomachs for the same reason. When I lead meditation sessions, I also typically begin by striking a gong three times – once for the Buddha, once for the Dharma, and once for the Sangha, or spiritual community.

I think it's important for seekers to remember that we can actually become awakened – enlightened – through conscious hearing. Milarepa, the enlightened Tibetan yogi, for example, is usually drawn with his hand cupped around his right ear to emphasize that he is listening to the sounds of the natural world – reading the book of nature, as it were. He's tuning in to the infinite through the finite sounds of nature. All of Milarepa's one hundred thousand songs came from true listening.

Chinese Buddhists have long celebrated the birthday of the Bodhisattva Kuan Yin, who is often depicted resembling an ethereal Chinese woman in flowing robes, not unlike Western depictions of Mary. There is a legend that says that Kuan Yin – whose name is translated as 'one who hears the cries of the world' – became enlightened because she *heard* and paid attention to the suffering of the world.

The Tibetan equivalent of Kuan Yin, of course, is Avalokitesvara, the androgynous Bodhisattva of limitless compassion. Anyone who studies Buddhism will hear a lot about Avalokitesvara. Probably the best known and loved of all Buddhist sutras is the brief, one-page Heart Sutra. The legend surrounding the Heart Sutra is that in the early days of Buddhism, the Buddha himself appeared in the guise of Avalokitesvara to teach the Heart Sutra to five hundred monks and nuns who were gathered at Vulture's Peak in Rajgir, about a half day's walk from the Bodhi Tree in Bodh Gaya. The story is that many of the monks became so upset at the uncompromising proclamation of absolute truth that they actually vomited. In short, they couldn't stomach the naked unadorned truth contained within this iconoclastic discourse on ultimate voidness; it shook them up and shattered their doctrinaire concepts. The Heart Sutra, of course, resonates all the way to the present as the essence of transcendental wisdom, reminding us that form is nothing but emptiness, and that emptiness shapes up as form.

When the Buddha taught the Heart Sutra, he appeared in the form of Avalokitesvara. Having meditated deeply on the source of all sound – in other words, the source of all arisings and appearances, all sights, sounds, feelings – Avalokitesvara realized the emptiness and ungraspability of these apparition-like appearances. This great Bodhisattva was thus released from clinging to materiality or concepts.

Avalokitesvara, who embodies compassion and love, awoke to the most profound wisdom of prajna paramita (transcendental wisdom) by awakening to the truth of pure hearing. He/she heard the true sounds of the universe and plumbed the source of all sound. When I talk about listening with the third ear, I don't mean the inner ear with those little bones and pieces. I mean the real ear of listening where we're really receiving, receptive, and sensitive. I mean really being touched by the world around us and the people we meet.

THE PRACTICE OF LISTENING BEGINS WITH SILENCE – A REFLECTION

Kabir, the medieval Indian sage and poet, sang, 'God hears even the bracelets jangling on the feet of a mosquito.'

What would it be like to have hearing so acute, so sensitive, so perfectly in tune with the world that we could hear everything – spoken and unspoken? Most of us are nowhere near that divine ideal; we're still struggling to hear our friends, partners, and children. We're struggling to hear the distinctions between truth and illusion in our own lives; we're still trying to learn how to listen.

Tibetan masters say there are three kinds of wisdom. First, there is hearing wisdom. That is followed by reflecting or contemplating wisdom, and then there is experiential meditative wisdom. In short, we listen and learn; then we reflect; and then we meditate and internalize. Throughout this process there is tremendous emphasis on hearing and listening.

To help us reflect on our capacity to listen and hear, Tibetan teachers often use the symbol of a cooking pot waiting to be filled with knowledge and wisdom that is nourishment for the spirit. There is even a teaching for sincere students to apply to themselves, called the Five Defects of a

Vessel. This teaching helps us reflect on conditions to avoid if we are to be suitable vessels for truth and wisdom.

The Five Defects of a Vessel

1. A POT WHICH IS TURNED OVER

When we are facing the wrong direction, we are essentially unavailable to even the most nourishing substances. This is a reminder that we get to choose which direction we face. We need to make wholesome choices and be available to hear wisdom teachings.

2. A POT WHICH IS COVERED

Have you ever tried to talk to somebody who is wearing earphones? In the same way, how can anything be poured into a vessel which, to all intents and purposes, is shut down? This reminds us to be receptive and open.

3. A POT THAT ALREADY CONTAINS SOMETHING POISONOUS

If we were to pour the purest water into a vessel that contained a toxic substance, although the toxin would be diluted, the water would still be corrupted. This reminds us to purify ourselves so that we are ready to receive.

4. A POT WHICH IS ALREADY FILLED TO THE BRIM

This symbol tells us not to be so full of ourselves and our opinions and ideas that there is no room for anything else.

5. A POT THAT LEAKS

We all know the expression 'in one ear, and out the other.' It is not enough to hear and be filled with wisdom; we need to learn how to retain it.

NOBLE SILENCE

Listening takes place not just through the ears, but with all the senses. Sometimes the best way to prepare ourselves to hear in a new and better way is to be still and silent. When we quiet our motor minds – and our motor mouths – we find that we are better able to open our hearts. The ancient practice of Noble Silence helps us begin the process of hearing in a new way; this is a timeless and wise practice that helps us be more sensitive and perceptive.

Noble Silence traditionally begins with a vow to keep silent for a specific period of time. It can be an hour, a day, a week, or a month. There are practitioners who have kept Noble Silence for years. There is even a practice of lifetime silence in India called 'maun.' The famous master Meher Baba was a mauni baba, a silent holy man. He used a small blackboard to spell out his succinct messages, like 'Don't worry, be happy,' long before the reggae song was written.

If you want to try a period of Noble Silence, remember that it is a rest for all of the senses. Turn off the radio, the phone, the television. Enjoy a fast from the news. Turn off the thoughts in your head. Stay quiet. Take refuge in the inner calm and peace of the quiet mind. Don't write, don't read, don't surf the Net. Keep still. Listen to the sounds around you. What do you hear? What do you see? Open your eyes, open your ears, open your heart. Think of the ancient Christian exercise. Be still. Listen to the inner voice, and know God. This is how we learn to cultivate higher levels of hearing, perception, and vision.

'For someone deeply trapped in a prison of thought, how good it can feel to meet a mind that hears, a heart that reassures. It's as if listening mind is, in and of itself, an invitation to another mind to listen too. How much it can mean when we accept the invitation and hear the world anew.'
— From *How Can I Help* by Ram Dass and Paul Gorman

CHAPTER SIX

The Connection Reflex –
Building Meaningful Relationships

While I was in Tibet . . . there was a certain degree of respect given to the office of the Dalai Lama and people related to me accordingly, regardless of whether they had true affection towards me or not. But if that was the only basis of people's relation to me, then when I lost my country, it would have been extremely difficult. But there is another source of worth and dignity from which you can relate to other fellow human beings. *You can relate to them because you are still a human being, within the human community. You share that bond. And that human bond is enough to give rise to a sense of worth and dignity. That bond can become a source of consolation in the event that you lose everything else.*

– His Holiness, the Dalai Lama

As the Dalai Lama points out, the human bond, the connectedness we share with each other, is an ever reliable source of strength and comfort. This is true for all of us. Anyone who is fortunate enough to have a friend or relative who is consistently supportive knows how much we depend on connections such as these. Anyone who has ever been seriously ill and had to go to the hospital remembers what it feels like to have a kind doctor, nurse, or medical technician stand by the side of the gurney. It isn't just the medical expertise that's comforting; it's the human presence that makes us feel that we are not alone. Anyone who has ever relied on a kind stranger to help at roadside with sudden car trouble knows why some people refer to these Samaritans as angels.

We all reach out automatically to connect, a little like new infants who reach out to curl their tiny hands around their mothers' fingers. I call it the *connection reflex*. Just as we need others, so too they need us. It's not a choice. 'No man is an island entire of itself,' as John Donne wrote. We are never disconnected from the whole. This intrinsic knowledge of our place in the greater picture is part of our spiritual DNA, our original software, or heartware. But the question that we as seekers need to ask ourselves is whether our relationships – our human connections – reflect our spiritual values and intentions. Are our interactions with others an expression of our inner goodness and nobility of heart? As we communicate, work, and play with others, are we remembering our commitment to integrate spirit into everything we do and say? Or are we just going through the motions, like automatons, or worse, using others for our own ends?

Our relationships precisely mirror our satisfaction, or lack of it, with life itself. When we are unhappy, most often it's because we don't have satisfying relationships. Not that long ago, a thirty-five-year-old man named Daniel came to talk to me. Daniel told me that he felt alienated – emotionally isolated and alone. Daniel felt that much of his dissatisfaction came from how he interacts with others. He felt as though he had never been able to make the human connections that would give his life meaning. 'Even in my marriage,' he said, 'I feel as though I am living with a stranger. I don't know my wife, and I don't feel that she knows me. Maybe it's me,' he continued, 'but I don't seem to be able to share my genuine feelings. Nor do I understand what it is that she's trying to communicate. The same thing is true in most of my other relationships as well. I sometimes feel as though it wouldn't matter to anyone whether I live or die.'

A large part of our spiritual work here on this planet is finding ways to heal these feelings of isolation and alienation in ourselves and in those we meet. We do this by placing a value on developing deeper connections as a way of enriching our lives and our world. A good life is not about money, real estate, careers, or the stock market; it's about how well we love and are loved. It's about living with heart.

INTEGRATING RELATIONSHIPS INTO OUR SPIRITUAL QUEST

As we work to incorporate our relationships into our spiritual quest, we are reminded that even the most classical Buddhist teachings are about relationship. When the Buddha, for example, set down his Noble Eight-fold Path to enlightenment, he talked about issues like friendliness and loving-kindness, positive intentions, ethics, wise speech, right livelihood, and right action. This has everything to do with relationship. The spiritual path isn't just about explicit religious formalities, rites, and rituals. Nor is it exclusively about mystical experience and meditative epiphanies. Most of it is simply about learning how to live an enlightened, loving life, day to day. The day-to-day antidote to alienation and loneliness is connection. The day-to-day practice or exercise that brings this about is reaching out and making genuine contact – touching and being touched.

As we go about our lives, we typically encounter and relate to many people – friends, family, and strangers. Whether these relationships are casual or intimate, we are given countless opportunities to apply the deeper values we believe in. We can put these opportunities into a spiritual framework by thinking of them as spiritual practices or exercises to help us train and strengthen our intentions.

Relating to others in a more spiritual fashion is a fairly simple and straightforward process; throughout human history, suggestions on how to do it have been given to us by the sages and masters of all the spiritual traditions. There is little that is new in the list that I'm including, but then there is nothing new under the sun; all we have are new opportunities to apply timeless wisdom every day of our marvelous lives.

CONNECTING AND REACHING OUT – HOW TO DO IT

Accept Others as They Are – Warts and All

When I started to think about this idea, I searched the word 'acceptance' on the Net to see what came up. I discovered large numbers of support groups formed by people who were struggling together to find acceptance. One such group, for example, was formed by people who are overweight, another by men and women who are gay. It was a sad reminder of how much intolerance there is in the world, and how much we all need to stop rejecting others for how they look, what they think, and who they are. I'm still shocked by the amount of intolerance and bigotry that still exists, even in this modern age; it seems as though every time I turn on the news, another example of it is highlighted. This is one of those 'When will we ever learn?' issues that we all need to address in our own lives.

The lesson of acceptance is an integral part of the spiritual path. Unconditional acceptance, after all, is about love; it's about opening our hearts and offering an unconditional 'yes' to the world. I was recently reading a book by the Benedictine monk and teacher Brother David Steindl-Rast, who writes, 'The "yes" of the human heart is our full response to the "faithfulness at the heart of all things." In saying this "yes," we become what we are. Our true self is "Yes."' *Yes,* I thought to myself. *Yes!* Brother David stirs my Buddhist heart.

As seekers, the question we need to ask ourselves is how can we effectively say 'yes' to the people around us? How can we appropriately convey acceptance and love? To get more insight into how to do this, think about the people, places, and situations that make you feel accepted. I have certain friends who I love to visit. When I walk through the door they convey a sense of great pleasure at having me there. In their homes I feel enveloped in warmth, friendship, and acceptance. We are connected, as if we are one family – one person, almost. This is spiritual connection – authentic relationship.

When we feel accepted, we feel as though we 'belong,' don't we? We feel as though we are on the same team; we have a place in the world, a purpose in being here; we feel aligned with others to whom we are connected in the most basic way. Therefore, doesn't it make sense that one of the simplest ways we can convey acceptance is by being inclusive and by helping others feel as though they belong as well? In short, we do this by saying *yes* to those we meet. We do this by including others in our thoughts, our prayers, and our actions; we do this by rooting out all the various shadowy forms of prejudice and intolerance in our own hearts. We do this by cultivating thoughts and wishes of well-being, loving-kindness, and compassionate concern for all that lives, breathes, and is.

The Dharma suggests that we can train ourselves to be more open and accepting of others by focusing first on the object of our greatest affection. Think about the warm feelings you have for your children or your grandparents or even your Siamese cat, for example. We continue to love and accept those we love, even though they are not always perfect. We train in loving-kindess by extending similar feelings to others, beginning with those we love the most and then working our way outward in ever-widening circles of spiritual embrace.

Let Go of Closed and Judgmental Points of View

If you have a problem, who do you want to talk to? Someone who listens to what you have to say with an open and loving attitude, or someone who greets you with a series of judgments and fixed opinions? Do you like to hang out with people who are critical and judgmental? I doubt it. If you're like most of us, most likely these are the people you try to avoid. Or perhaps you try to straighten such people out – which most likely implies trying to bring them around to your point of view. Good luck!

My friend Anna sometimes complains about her cousin, Rosie, who is known throughout the family as 'Rosie, the critic.' Anna says, 'I love Rosie, but I can't stand spending time with her. From the minute she walks through my door all she does is criticize. "Why did you sauté the vegetables instead of steaming them? Why are your children wearing torn sneakers? You need a different haircut; why don't you go to my stylist? Why don't you do something about the broken tile on the kitchen floor?"' According to Anna, Rosie can't stop herself. Nothing ever pleases her; she notes every imperfection and finds fault with everything and everyone who crosses her path. Anna says that she and Rosie once went to a restaurant; at the door, the maître d' stopped them before they sat down, saying that Rosie had sent so many meals back to the kitchen that they would prefer that she not eat there anymore.

Of course, at least a little part of each of us is like 'Rosie, the critic.' I call this part *the inner tyrant*. The inner tyrant always thinks it knows; it's never totally satisfied, and nothing is ever quite good enough to meet its perfectionistic standards. We all have at least a few days or periods when the inner tyrant rules. When we're being severely judgmental, of course, we're losing sight of Bodhicitta, our loving intentions to express compassion and tolerance to everyone we meet.

Usually a critical attitude reflects a lack of self-acceptance. Our inner tyrant often most harshly judges ourselves. One way we can start to work on our judgmental attitudes is by softening up, cutting ourselves some slack, and showing ourselves more love and kindness. Using spiritual intelligence we can remind ourselves that in the greater scheme of things, today's critical opinions have very little significance.

DO UNTO OTHERS AS YOU WOULD HAVE OTHERS DO UNTO YOU

Professor John Makransky, my close friend and colleague, always has wonderful stories to share about the experience of parenting his two small sons. The other evening, John was downstairs in his house working when five-year-old Jonathan came to say goodnight. 'Did you brush your teeth?', John asked his son.

'Yes,' Jonathan answered.

'Very good,' said John. 'Now, did you brush your feet?'

'No, Daddy. I didn't brush my feet.' Jonathan looked confused.

'Well,' John said, 'you had better go upstairs and tell Mommy that you brushed your teeth, but you haven't brushed your feet yet.'

So Jonathan, who was in pajamas with bare feet, started walking up the stairs slowly. Meanwhile he was thinking . . . thinking.

When Jonathan got to the top of the stairs, he stopped. Instead of going into the room his mother was in, he turned and looked back at his father. 'Daddy,' he said, 'what do you mean "brush my feet?" You're teasing me, aren't you?'

'Yes, Jonathan,' John replied. 'I am teasing you.'

Jonathan put his hands on his waist and shook his head disapprovingly. 'Please don't do that any more, Daddy,' he said. 'Put yourself in my place. How would *you* feel?'

From the mouths of babes, wisdom flows. The lesson is crystal clear: Whatever we do, whatever we say, all we have to think is how we would want to be treated. From this concept emerges a natural sense of morality as well as caring, unselfish, ethical behavior. Jesus said, 'Do to others as you would have them do to you.'

The Buddha said:

> *'See yourself in others*
> *Then whom can you hurt?*
> *What harm can you do?'*

★

DEVELOP AN AUTHENTICALLY
GENEROUS SPIRIT

'The more we have, the more we have to give.'

Generosity starts in the mind, with an intention to be more sincerely giving and open-hearted. The Buddha once told a follower that generosity was so important that we shouldn't sit down to a single meal without sharing it in some way. In Tibet every monk, nun, and lama begins each meal by first taking a portion of food, often rice, wadding it into a ball and throwing it outside or placing it aside to feed the hungry spirits. In this way, we are reminded of the value of sharing as well as of the depth of pain that can be suffered by those whose lives are dominated by either hunger or greed.

Giving, of course, doesn't always come naturally. That's why the Buddha once told a wealthy, but stingy, businessman that he should train himself in the virtue of generosity. The Buddha suggested that the man think of his two hands – right and left – as being separate entities, one of them poor and the other wealthy. The Buddha told the businessman to learn how to 'let go' and give by taking a coin in the 'wealthy hand' and giving it to the 'poor hand.' The Buddha told him that he should experiment with increasingly larger sums of money and greater objects of wealth until he was able to cultivate nonattachment and give generously and freely to others too.

The act of sharing means that we are beginning to let go of our clinging and greed; we are loosening our tendency to hang onto whatever we have. There are many different kinds of things, both outer and inner, that we can give. We can learn to let go on many levels; some of our most valuable gifts, of course, are inner gifts of spirit and love, which are best enjoyed by being shared. The more we have, the more we have to give. And the more we can give, the more we receive, as everyone knows.

The first principle of Buddhism's Six Principles of Enlightened Living is the perfection of generosity, which in Sanskrit is called 'Dana Paramita.' Dana is the wisdom of openness – internal, external, and innate. This means open hands, open arms, open mind, and open heart. When we share our bounty, in whatever form, with others, we are following through on our intention not to be greedy or selfish; we are following through on our intention to connect with the world.

Thinking about Dana Paramita reminds us that it's wise to let go. It is simply in our own higher self-interest. Externally, generosity implies being more open, giving, service-oriented, and unselfish with our material goods, energy, and time. Internally, it's about not being miserly with our emotions and our love, but being more open-hearted. Innately, just *being* represents innate generosity. Everything is available in the natural state of pure being. There is inexhaustible abundance and glory within, so exploit your own inner natural resources.

Here are some of the ways we can share our bounty:

✳ SHARING MONEY AND GIFTS

There are some common reasons why it can be difficult to give. When we give others money or material objects of any kind, for example, it presupposes that there will be less left over for us. Just this morning, a friend was visiting me and asked if I had anything to drink. 'I don't know,' I said. 'Look in the refrigerator.' 'Is it okay if I finish the orange juice?' my friend asked. 'Sure,' I replied. As I said yes, I had a knee-jerk reaction: It crossed my mind that there would be no orange juice for breakfast the next day. And for a second, I wanted to 'hang on' – not 'let go' of my single serving of juice. Most of us know the feeling, don't we? I mean, the truth is that in my fortunate life, there is plenty of orange juice just up the street, not to mention the various kinds of tea in my cupboard to get me through tomorrow morning – so where is the resistance really coming from?

As seekers who are trying to be more free and generous, we know that we are working on the deepest forms of giving; we are cultivating our capacity to open up, let go, and give with a genuinely open heart. In short, while sharing the orange juice is nice and a good thing, it would be wonderful if we could also be happy and grateful for the opportunity to share. Giving often creates choices. Let's say you have $200 worth of discretionary income left in your wallet, and you really would like to buy a new jacket. Walking past a store window, you see a nice looking jacket. You think, *I'd look good in that. I'd feel good in that.* But wait, you remember that a friend is having a birthday. You'd like to be able to do something special as a celebration. And your mother's radio just broke; as much as she loves listening to the radio, you know she's so worried about money that she won't buy herself a new one. And your brother and his wife are having a hard time right now; they're saving up to send your nephew to camp for the summer, and every little bit makes a difference. And your mailbox is also filled with letters from worthwhile organizations asking you to contribute to campaigns to help others. So I guess you will have to make a decision about whether to help others or buy yourself a piece of clothing. These are choices that we make.

✳ GIVE THE GIFT OF TIME AND ENERGY

Time is often the most precious commodity. When we use our time to do something for someone else, we might have less left over for ourselves. Who has enough time and energy to do everything? I know I don't. In my life, I personally am always facing the time dilemma. The phone rings. On the answering machine, I hear a student who wants me to explain part of one of my Monday night Boston Dharma talks; on the television is a basketball game that I would love to sit down and enjoy. This is a time choice I often have to make. In my own case, I'm a Dharma teacher. When I was in Asia in my twenties and thirties, my own spiritual masters were extraordinarily generous with their teachings, their time, and their energy. I'm always aware of this. When I asked them how I could repay their kindness to me, they said, 'Pass it on.' I consider this my responsibility.

How are you asked to give time regularly? Do you have children who would like to spend more time with you? A wife, husband or romantic partner? Do you have a friend who wants you to help her move? Do you know someone in a nursing home or hospital who would appreciate a visit? or an elderly neighbor who needs help in shopping or getting to the doctor? Are you a member of a spiritual community that needs help with a fundraiser or a specific project? In our time-starved modern society, making a conscious commitment of time and energy is always a beautiful gift.

✳ BE KIND

Think about the people in your life who have given you the gift of kindness. What is it they did that made you appreciate them? I asked some people to give me examples of kindness that had been extended to them. Here's what they said:

✳ Martha described a childhood music teacher who was *gentle* in her criticism and *encouraging* in her praise.

✳ Ed remembered the man whose new car he had recently sideswiped; he said the man *smiled* understandingly and tried to make Ed feel better about what had happened.

✳ Barbara talked about a friend who always has a kind and *supportive* word for everyone.

✳ Doug was particularly touched by the veterinarian who wrote him a letter of *sympathy* when his dog died and made a contribution in the dog's memory to a veterinarian hospital.

Kindness is an extraordinary quality. Those who are able to embody it have learned how not to be stingy with words, encouragement, and love. Those of us who are on the receiving end of kindness are always made a little bit better by the experience. Eric Hoffer said, 'We are made kind by being kind.'

✳ GIVE ENERGY AND COURAGE

I'm impressed by people who choose potentially lifesaving occupations that routinely require great energy and sometimes even greater courage. Firemen, of course, are one of the most obvious examples. Medical missionaries and emergency medical and rescue workers are others.

About a year ago, I read an obituary in the *New York Times* for a man I had never met, but I wish I had. The obituary headline read, 'Adrian Marks, a Navy pilot who rescued 56 sailors struggling in the shark-filled Philippine Sea after the cruiser Indianapolis was sunk by Japanese torpedoes in July 1945.'

The obituary said that Mr Marks, who was eighty-one when he died, was a lieutenant during the Second World War. In that role, Lieutenant Marks, on a routine mission on a sunny day piloting a seaplane that was meant to land only in calm water, flew over American survivors of a torpedo attack in high and dangerous seas. Ignoring orders, and with the agreement and support of his crew members, Lieutenant Marks risked both his life and his crew's by putting his plane down in the midst of twelve-foot swells.

Because he did this, the plane essentially became a life raft, no longer able to take off; in short, Marks and his crew sacrificed their freedom to help others. They put as many men in their plane as they could, and then used parachute material to tie others on the wings, which were bobbing up and down on the ocean. That's how they spent the night until help came the following day. After the war, Marks went on to open a law practice in Indiana. In 1975, there was a reunion of the survivors of that event, and Marks spoke, paying tribute to the men with whom he had shared this terrifying experience. 'I met you thirty years ago,' he said. 'I met you on a sparkling, sun-swept afternoon of horror. I have known you through a balmy tropic night of fear. I will never forget you.'

I was very moved by this story; it reminded me that courageousness in caring for others has always been viewed as a Bodhisattva activity. In ancient Indian Buddhist scriptures, Bodhisattvas are likened to snow white geese, who dive down even into the depths of hell to deliver suffering creatures from pain, torment, and fear as if they were diving down into a lake. Most of us will never be called upon to literally save a human life, but most of us do have some opportunities to be fearless when it comes to saving the lives of animals and insects. And sooner or later, most of us will have opportunities to be brave enough to put our comfort and security at risk by helping other human beings. This is a way of being generous.

There are many ways to help save another's life. Not that long ago I saw a story on the news about a delivery man in New York City who had taken it upon himself to help a street person whom he regularly saw on the streets. This was a homeless alcoholic man whose mother went to church every Sunday and prayed for word of her son. The delivery man, clearly an urban Bodhisattva, spent several years giving the homeless man small amounts of money for food, trying to gain his trust in order to find out who he was and if he had any family. Finally he was able to get him to reveal a phone number, and he helped place him in a detox program and helped reunite him with his family. The two men attended a church service together, and the former street person, who was a talented musician, played a hymn for the man who was helping him find his way off the streets.

In truth, we all need at least a little bit of saving. So look around. Whose life can you help save today? Sometimes it just takes a few kind words. God saves those who save one another.

✳ SHARE WHAT YOU KNOW

My friend Lorraine recently told me that she is incredibly grateful to the instructor who helped her learn how to ski. Her instructor was so skillful and encouraging that, despite her fears, after just a few lessons, Lorraine is now actually enjoying gliding down the mountain on her new short skis, something she thought she would never be able to do.

Don't we all feel gratitude when someone takes the time to share with us what they know? Information is wealth, and not everybody is open-hearted enough to share what they know. In fact, some people hoard their information, preferring to maintain an elitist position that restricts learning and information to the chosen few – no matter what the subject. An ancient Buddhist text says that if you know where to go to read Buddhist sutras and if because of stinginess, you don't share this information with others, you run the risk of being reborn as an earthworm. So take care! You don't want to spend a lifetime with a mouthful of dirt ascending toward the surface light.

It seems as though there is often someone who takes the 'I know something you don't know' attitude. We see this in all areas of expertise; maybe that's why we appreciate those who offer us information that helps us become knowledgeable. Knowledge is like freeware; it belongs to everyone.

I'm very grateful to the various friends who helped me learn how to use a computer; I'm grateful to the high school teacher who first turned me on to the joys of poetry; I'm grateful to my mother for helping me learn how to drive a car, leaving me with a series of vivid memories I will never forget; I'm grateful to the counselor in summer camp who taught me how to swim and dive; I'm grateful to my father who taught me how to ride and balance myself on a bicycle, cajoling me into not being overly nervous. And of course, I am incredibly grateful to my kind Buddhist teachers, many of whom were Tibetan refugee monks living in extremely difficult circumstances; nonetheless, they taught me how to find spiritual sanity and a more profound balance. We all have teachers in our lives to whom we are grateful. We can repay our gratitude by 'passing it on' and unstintingly sharing what we know.

✳ GIVE THE GIFT OF DHARMA

All Buddhist teachings say that the greatest gift we can give anyone is the gift of Dharma. 'Dharma' is a Sanskrit word with many meanings. It can be translated as teaching, truth, doctrine, religion, spirituality, or reality. The literal meaning is 'that which supports or upholds.' Dharma also means 'that which heals.'

There is an old Japanese Buddhist story that I like about a master who begged daily to raise large sums of money in order to build a temple in which people could be edified by learning Dharma. However, when the time finally came for the temple to be built, there was a famine in the land, and people were starving. Instead of building the large temple he had imagined, the master turned all the money over to the people for food. Bodhicitta, the altruistic intention to alleviate suffering and bring about spiritual deliverance, is constant and unswerving, yet the ways and means can and must be flexible enough to adapt and change.

When we give the gift of Dharma, we are giving others what they need most, whatever that might be. Therefore, if we share what we have genuinely learned through life experience and what we know about spiritual teachings, we are giving Dharma. Moreover if we are able to give someone wise advice, we are also giving someone the gift of Dharma. Often just by listening to someone's troubles, we are giving the gift of Dharma, by lending them an ear as a sounding board or a shoulder to lean on.

People in this postmodern, cynical age are often embarrassed about admitting their spiritual interest or sharing their personal spiritual treasures. Many have told me, however, that when they open up and talk with others about what's really meaningful, they discover that they are not alone. When we share Dharma, we connect on the deepest levels.

✳ BECOME A GENEROUS 'RECEIVER'

When Deidra was getting ready to move, she opened a closet and packed the leather briefcase that her late employer had given her once when she had been promoted. Deidra loved the briefcase, and had been very touched by the gift when she received it. However, years later, Deidra realizes that she never really conveyed her feelings to her old boss. Now, with the wisdom of hindsight, Deidra wonders why she had been so stingy with her thanks.

It's often just as important to receive with an open heart as it is to give. By definition, relationships of all kinds have to do with reciprocity and mutuality. Relationships that fall apart often do so because they are out of balance; they experience ratio strain. In her relationship with her friend Margo, Fredda is fed up because she feels as though she always gives, gives, gives. Margo, on the other hand, thinks that Fredda never allows Margo to give those things that she can. There is always an interesting connection between giver and recipient. Some people, for example, prefer the role of caretaker; they are uncomfortable when someone tries to take care of them, and they sort of 'hijack' all the giving in a relationship. The thing to remember is that giver and receiver are building good karma together, so give someone else a chance to give.

Think about how much pleasure and joy we get when we give a present to a child who is truly excited and happy about receiving it. We were probably all better receivers when we were children. Nonetheless, being a good receiver is an art that's worth relearning. Say thank you. Be appreciative. Show your joy. Feel it.

EMPATHIZE WITH OTHERS

A few years back, I was with a friend who was picking up a small child from preschool. While I waited for my friend and his son, I watched a little drama unfold. One toddler – she couldn't have been more than two or three – was crying because she didn't want to leave the fingerpainting she had been working on to go home. The teacher and the child's parents were all trying to reason with her, but the little girl was having none of it. Suddenly another little boy, her own size, who already had his coat on, broke away from his mother and ran over to the sobbing child; he put his arms around her shoulders. 'Don't cry, Sarah,' he said. 'You can finish it tomorrow. I'll help you. Please don't cry.' He sounded as though he felt her unhappiness with almost as much intensity as she did. His behavior reminded me of the stories told of Tibet's little Bodhisattvas – children called 'tulkus,' who are the reincarnation of previous spiritual masters; these little budding Buddhas seem naturally able to feel and respond to another's pain. Inside each of us is a tender and sensitive little Buddha who is naturally able to empathize with anyone. We can reconnect with that underlying tenderheartedness in us, no matter how old and hardened we have become.

STAY OPEN AND CHALLENGE
YOUR ASSUMPTIONS

My friend Patti is an animal lover. She says that people, therefore, assume that she is prepared to baby-sit for all kinds of creatures. That's why when a friend of hers had to be hospitalized, Patti was called upon to take care of his African gray parrot, Gwendolyn. Patti had never taken care of a bird before, and she had certainly never tried to forge a relationship with one. Gwendolyn's owner, a day trader, had always told Patti that his parrot was an amazing creature who could speak in sentences and respond appropriately to all kinds of stimuli. Nonetheless, Patti was surprised by the range of the bird's vocabulary. The first time she put together a pile of clothes to be washed and walked past the parrot's cage with a laundry bag, the bird squawked, 'laundry day . . . laundry day.' And when she put on MSNBC on the television for the news during the day, and the ticker tape information ran across the screen, the bird yelled out, 'Nasdaq. Nasdaq.' Perhaps he had some stock tips!

Maybe Gwendolyn was only parroting, but she certainly used words appropriately. Over the next few weeks Patti and Gwendolyn became friends. Patti shared her breakfast with Gwendolyn every morning because she loved feeding Gwendolyn bits of toast and egg or cereal and hearing the bird say, 'hmmmm . . . very good.' When the bird's owner, Michael, was finally well enough to take the bird home, he came to pick her up. When Gwendolyn saw him, she yelled 'Michael' and jumped up and down. Then when he came near the cage, Gwendolyn seemed to remember that she was angry at him for leaving her, and she looked the other way whenever he tried to talk to her, giving him the cold shoulder – or feathers, as it were. Finally Michael coaxed Gwendolyn out of her cage. When she was standing on his arm, the parrot couldn't stay angry any longer. She jumped up on her owner's shoulder and buried her little face in his neck. 'Hello,' she cried. 'Hello!'

When Gwendolyn left with Michael for her own home, Patti observed the parrot's great happiness and relief at being reunited with her owner, and yet Patti was genuinely sorry to see her leave. They had become such great friends (birds of a feather . . .)

So what's the point of this story about a highly articulate parrot? Just that we all tend to make assumptions about other beings, no matter what species those beings belong to. We assume that we couldn't possibly develop a relationship with the bird that sits outside our window. We don't even think of the bird as having 'feelings,' even though we know that birds do form bonds. So too, we often assume that we couldn't become friends with the hundreds of people we meet each year who are somehow 'different' from us.

Whenever we stereotype a group or a gender, we are making assumptions. Men often assume that women will not fully appreciate team sports, for example, which is simply not true. Women assume other things about men, I am sure – I am just not always sure what! We decide arbitrarily that people who are older, younger, richer, or poorer are different from us and couldn't possibly fit into our lives. We assume the same things about people who have more or less education than we do. Our prejudices deprive our lives of richness and texture; these assumptions leave us with fewer possibilities for making joyous connections in our daily lives.

BE 'PRESENT' FOR OTHERS

'I'm Here for You'

My friend Clara recently told me that she uttered that sentence to another friend, a man who was experiencing serious personal and health problems. When she said it, what she meant was that she was prepared to 'show up' for whatever was needed. She was prepared to listen to her friend talk about the troubles he was experiencing; she was prepared to drive her friend to his doctor appointments; she was prepared to simply come and sit in his living room, simply offering her 'being' for support, comfort, and warmth.

Being able to just be authentically present and accounted for in our relationships is a deeply caring spiritual act. When my grandmother was in her late eighties, she was in a nursing home in Long Beach, Long Island. She was sort of losing her marbles and couldn't remember much. But I could see that as far as she was concerned, my just being with her in the present was totally and absolutely fine. I noticed that some people in my family had trouble with the fact that she couldn't remember where I lived, my name, and other such details. When I'd visit her with my local relatives, they kept trying to remind her. 'This is your oldest grandson, Jeffrey. You remember Jeffrey. He lives in France now and came all the way to see you.' My grandmother didn't care about France and couldn't remember my way of life. But while I was there, for those grand hours we shared, we were totally together. She knew who I was as her beloved grandson, even without such a title or label, and there we were in those moments together – totally there. All of our lifetime interconnections together had boiled down to that, and it was more than enough. It was exquisite. I loved visiting with her, sad as it could occasionally become.

That sort of sums up all of our lives, I think. If you strip away all the stories, beliefs, and fantasies, and unveil our vital, pulsing, living core, here we are, right now. We are here for ourselves; here for each other – just here. There is a symmetry, a rightness, and justness to this elemental fact.

USING THE POWER OF WORDS
TO BUILD DEEPER CONNECTIONS

Recently I was in an airport in San Francisco, waiting for a flight to Los Angeles. I had an extra half hour, so I went to a phone booth to check my home messages and make a few calls. As I stood there, talking on the phone, the woman in the next booth hung up the phone, looked at me, and said, 'I'm going to New Zealand for six months, and my husband just told me that the car broke down, and he wants to know what he should do.' She separated her hands and looked up to the heavens with a do-you-believe-it expression, and after we shared a nod, she hurried away.

If only for a moment, this New Zealand–bound woman needed to connect; she needed to talk and vent her feelings, even to a stranger. She needed to share her private little joke about the absurdities of life. And she did; we had our fifteen seconds of connection together. The connections we make with others, both superficial and profound, most often begin with the spoken word. As the first sentence in the New Testament book of John states, 'In the beginning was the word.'

We use words to convey what we think; we use words to express how we feel. When we are trying to deepen our connections or resolve differences, we typically use the power of the spoken or written word. More often than not, what we say and how we say it determines the quality of any relationship.

The Buddha was so sensitive to the power of words that one step of the Noble Eight-fold Path is called Right Speech, or Impeccable Communication. The Buddha instructed his followers to speak the truth simply, without adornment; he exhorted them to speak honestly; he told them to use their words in gentle, peace-loving ways that reflect inner wisdom, clear vision, and their intentions to help, not harm, others.

Words come in different forms and languages, from a baby's first words to power words like mantras to nonsense words like those in Lewis Carroll's classic poem 'Jabberwocky.' We use so many words every day, and we use them in so many ways – helpfully, harmfully, lovingly, cruelly, consciously, and unconsciously. We use words to speak to others, and we also use words to speak to ourselves – not just walking down the street, talking to the air, but in our incessant internal monologues. Not that long ago I saw a cartoon of a large stout Buddha, modeled on the large meditating stone Buddha overlooking the sea in Kamakura, Japan. The thought bubble coming out of the Buddha's head said, 'I hate my thighs.' Who knows, maybe even Buddhas talk to themselves.

Conscious Speech/Conscious Relationships

What we say to ourselves shapes the relationship we have with ourselves. And what we say to others shapes our relationships with the rest of the world. If there is one thing that any one of us could do that would automatically improve the quality of our relationships, it would be to become more conscious of what we say and how we say it. All of our relationships will be changed and transformed when we change and transform ourselves in this way. I guarantee it.

Have you ever had the experience of really wanting to say something that you considered important, and then not having the courage to speak your mind? Have you ever said anything you later deeply regretted? Of course you have; we all have. Not that long ago I spoke to a woman named Nancy who was incredibly upset because of a conversation she'd had with her mother an hour before her mother suffered a serious heart attack. Nancy said that her mother had been obviously upset and kept complaining of indigestion. Nancy was trying to finish a work-related project when her mother called. Because she was feeling pressured, Nancy said, she had been abrupt and not particularly sympathetic to what her mother was saying. In this case, Nancy's mother recovered, and Nancy was fortunate to have more opportunities to be a loving daughter. However, this experience showed her how important it is to be mindful and aware in all her conversations and interactions, with everybody.

An important reason for staying conscious in our speech is to avoid later regrets. Barbara says she still cringes when she remembers the time she yelled at her daughter, saying, 'You're so stupid! How could you be so stupid?' Martin says that his marriage has never quite recovered from the time he told his wife, 'If you don't lose some weight, I'm going to go out and find myself a skinny gal.' He says he was just teasing; to his wife, however, his words felt hurtful and threatening and lingered long in her memory. Ted says that he feels that he often hurts others with his words. He has a quick tongue and a sharp sense of humor. It's easy to take a quick poke at somebody just to get a laugh. One of his biggest challenges is learning how to restrain himself. I myself often find that words seem to just tumble off my tongue, so I try to pay attention and be careful of my mouth.

We can use words skillfully or unconsciously; we can use words to heal or to hurt. As seekers, our intention is to help, not harm. Our words can help us fulfill our highest intentions. I think it would really help all of us if, before we speak, we could stop for just a moment to make certain that what we are about to say accurately reflects our heart's intentions.

A DAY OF RIGHT SPEECH –
A HEALING PRACTICE

'May this day of right speech bring gentle blessings to those round me; may the blessings extend throughout the world.'

We start this practice by designating a day that will be devoted to using our words to fulfill our highest spiritual aspirations. It might be easiest to begin with a weekend, a Saturday or Sunday when there is likely to be less work-related stress and fewer deadlines or office politics. Here are some suggestions for things you can do:

✳ Put a Post-it note beside your bed the night before to remind yourself that this will be a day of 'Impeccable Speech.'

✳ Start the day with a heartfelt prayer that reaffirms your intention to always speak with compassion and love.

✳ Center and collect yourself each time you speak. Be mindful of all your words. Even if you want to say something as banal as 'please pass the mashed potatoes,' be conscious of your tone of voice, and whether you are saying what you really want to say.

✳ Find ways to keep your words gentle, loving, accurate, and positive. Do this even if you are annoyed and upset.

✳ See if you can discover better ways to talk to others that will open up new channels of communication.

✳ Don't lie and don't use words to manipulate or control others.

✳ Don't gossip.

✳ Don't say anything about anyone that you wouldn't say if that person were present.

✳ Use your words to encourage those around you.

✳ Express your most positive thoughts and feelings. Tell others that you care about them.

✳ Don't chatter; don't use words just to fill empty spaces with noise.

✳ Don't become nervous about the absence of speech; allow yourself and others to be silent.

✳ Cultivate a way of speaking that is simple and spare.

✳ Don't interrupt others; let the people around you finish their sentences and express their thoughts.

✳ Use your words to convey patience.

✳ Use your words to help your loved ones feel nourished and supported.

✳ Use your words to express gentleness and kindness.

✳ Try to make at least one person feel better because of something you say.

✳ Use your words to convey friendship, encouragement, and support.

✳ Try to phone and connect with at least one loved one with whom you have lost touch.

✳ Write a note to someone you care about, expressing your positive feelings.

✳ Take the time to express support for someone else's work or personal project.

✳ Think about the people you know who have suffered losses. Take the time today to write notes expressing your sympathy and empathy.

A day of right speech can only help your karma. Keep up the good word.

CHAPTER SEVEN

Finding Our Sacred Place in Nature

In relation to the earth, we have been autistic for centuries. Only now have we begun to listen with some attention and with a willingness to respond to the earth's demands that we cease our industrial assault, that we abandon our inner rage against the conditions of our earthly existence, that we renew our human participation in the grand liturgy of the universe.

– Thomas Berry

Nature provides ample evidence that we live in a cause-and-effect universe. Plant some tulip bulbs in the fall; watch as the graceful flowers make us smile come the spring. Throw chemicals into a stream or river, see the marine life die and the water and nearby soil become contaminated. As we begin to clean up a dangerously polluted waterway, fish start to return – but even so, they are often still dangerously toxic for human consumption.

Everything has consequences; being aware of this, we watch as karma unfolds.

Many of us spend our lives in areas where we are very insulated from a day-to-day awareness of what we are doing to the planet we live on. A few years ago, I heard a story about an eight-year-old New York boy named Johnny who joined the Cub Scouts and went away with his troop on a weekend camping trip to the Adirondacks. When Johnny returned, his father asked him how he had enjoyed himself.

'It was great!' Johnny replied. 'And we found a cow's nest in the woods.'

'A cow's nest?' His father was bemused and perplexed. 'But cows don't have nests.'

'Well,' Johnny said, 'we took a walk in the woods and we went to this place where there was a big pile of old broken milk bottles.'

Living, as we do, in a world filled with synthetics of all kinds, it's easy to become as misinformed about cause and effect as little Johnny. We forget that we are all dependent on the earth for food and clean water. We open our freezers to remove plastic bags, which we then pop into the microwave. Voilà, minutes later we cut open the plastic and squeeze out the helping of macaroni and ersatz cheese made with soy milk and chemicals. It looks good. It even tastes okay. The subliminal message we are receiving is that food comes from freezers, wrapped in plastic.

Because we feel removed from direct contact with our food supply, we are dependent on others to take care of us. We assume that scientists, politicians, and 'people in charge' will be responsible about issues like keeping our food and water supply safe. Yet of course, we also know that large businesses hire lobbyists and public relations experts, and spend fortunes making certain that senators and congressmen place more value on financial interests than they do on certain matters that affect our health and our humanity; ethical considerations are just forgotten. We have seen time and time again how often science fails Spiritual Intelligence 101 by being unwilling to take the long view or perceive the whole picture. There is an assumption that 'tomorrow' will take care of the problems we are creating today.

Recently, I read an article in the *New York Times* discussing some of the reasons why wild salmon are disappearing around the world. The possible causes are many: overfishing, changing climate and water temperatures, genetic weakening. Many believe that farm-bred salmon are creating many of the problems for various reasons. Some escape from their farm pens and get into waterways, and because they are weaker and smaller than the other salmon they may be genetically creating a weaker species. Another possible reason speaks to common sense: When the farm salmon are penned up together in close quarters, diseases and parasites can run amuck, attacking and killing the fish. These multiplying parasites can then spread to wild salmon. Another reason may be that the salmon's natural predators, such as seals, have increased. Whatever the reason, the disappearance of wild salmon provides an interesting example of cause and effect problems that scientists didn't anticipate would be exacerbated when salmon began to be farmed.

There are thousands of examples such as this. Did science accurately predict the illnesses that would be caused by radioactive fallout? Is torturing innocent animals in the name of science really necessary? Sometimes all that is being achieved is a cosmetic product. Did anyone fully anticipate the new and powerful bacterial strains that would emerge as a result of antibiotic use? Friends of mine in New York City are very concerned about the possibly toxic nature of the spray that has been used in the city to combat mosquitoes; they tell me that the spray killed not only the mosquitoes but also the monarch butterflies who were beginning their yearly migration to Mexico.

From the shrinking rain forest to radioactive waste, one could, of course, go on all day in this vein, pointing out tragic examples of man's damaging effect on the planet. Ultimately, of course, this destruction reverberates back on us all, affecting, among other things, global weather patterns and the very air we breathe. We know that there are environmental factors implicated in diseases from asthma to cancer. We're aware of the effects pesticides and chemicals have on the health of our young children. Why aren't we behaving accordingly?

The Buddha was very conscious of ecological issues even during his lifetime. He told his monks that they should each plant at least one tree every year to replace the ones that had been lost by human use. He also issued an edict telling his monks not to urinate near rivers or streams for fear of pollution. The Buddha had a special connection to trees. He was born under a tree with his mother grasping a branch; he became enlightened under a tree; and he died under a tree. If the Buddha were to appear today in Bodh Gaya near the Bodhi Tree where he realized perfect enlightenment, he wouldn't recognize the spot. During his lifetime, it was a lush forest wilderness, teeming with life. Today that section of northern India has been deforested and much of the area is now an arid desert.

We walk on common ground. That means all of us — all the peoples of all nations and all the creatures, large and small. As the earth's tenants, we have a spiritual and sacred obligation to try to become better stewards of the planet we call home. This is part of the rent we should be paying for a safer, well-preserved world. Whenever we ignore what we are doing to the earth, we do so at our own peril. We will suffer the consequences of our disregard and disrespect; so will our children and our children's children. The earth is our home. It belongs to all of us. Native Americans chant, 'The earth is our mother.' Right now, Mom needs our help. Unselfish service is the rent we can pay for a better world and a better life.

In Buddhism, we talk a great deal about being awake to reality and how it works. One of the major areas in which we *all* need to be a little more conscious and awake is in how we handle our relationships with the natural world. I know that I am not always as mindful about ecological concerns as I would like to be; very few of us are. I don't always recycle as diligently as I should; I don't always take the time to buy and use environmentally safe cleaning products. I'm trying to be more assiduous about this. As we become more conscious and make more intelligent choices, we see more clearly how our careless behavior has an effect on the whole. Native Americans, who had a more intimate relationship with the land, knew that if we touch any part of this universal web we inhabit, the whole world web shakes.

LOVING THE CREATURES OF THE EARTH

'. . . how terribly arrogant we have become because of a mistaken belief that man has dominion over the birds of the air and the fish of the seas. The word "dominion" was actually a translation of the Hebrew word "stewardship."'

— Jane Goodall

The natural world provides multitudinous opportunities for practices that reflect the compassion and caring of a Bodhisattva. There is a wonderful story that's told in Tibet about an old lama who would come every day to meditate on a large rock near a calm pond. Yet, no sooner would he cross his legs, settle down, and begin his prayers and devotions than he would spot some little insect struggling in the water. Time after time, he would lift up his thin, creaky old body, catch the insect gently in his hand, and carry it to the safety of a nearby plant. The minute he settled down again, the same thing would happen.

His fellow monks, who also went off every day to meditate alone in the rocky Tibetan countryside, noticed what he was doing. Some of them became quite concerned. How could the old lama get any meditating done when all his time was spent plucking tiny insects from the placid pool? As Tibetan Buddhists, they also recognized the wisdom in saving the life of any sentient being, no matter how tiny. But still, some of them wondered if the old monk should stop meditating by the pond and move somewhere where there were fewer distractions.

One day several of them finally approached him to give their opinions and advice. 'Wouldn't it be better,' one asked, 'if you could meditate undisturbed during the day? That way you would find perfect enlightenment more quickly and would then be able to free all living beings from the ocean of conditioned existence.'

'If you want to meditate by the pond,' another suggested, 'why don't you do so with your eyes closed?'

'How,' one of the youngest monks asked, 'can you hope to develop perfect tranquility and deep diamond-like concentration if you keep hopping up and down all day long?'

The wise old lama listened quietly. Finally he bowed and spoke. 'I'm sure my meditation would be deeper and more productive if I sat unmoved all day, just as you say my friends. But how can an old worthless one like myself, who has vowed again and again to devote this lifetime, and all his lives, to serving and liberating others, just sit with closed eyes and hardened heart, praying and intoning the altruistic mantra of Great Compassion, while right before my very eyes helpless creatures are drowning?'

To that simple humble question, none of the other monks could find an answer.

When we open our eyes and look around us, we see that many of the planet's creatures are suffering, and need our attention. Some men and women, with beautifully soft hearts, are particularly sensitive to the suffering of helpless animals. I know animal rescue people who go out daily to feed homeless dogs and cats. They spend their own money to take in these animals, who they neuter and spay before trying to find them good homes. This requires enormous effort. Some dog lovers volunteer at shelters where there are always needy dogs who are living in cages, waiting to be adopted; the absence of exercise increases the suffering of these animals, so volunteer dog walkers are particularly appreciated. There are also groups that rescue farm animals such as horses and donkeys and goats that are about to be destroyed often because they are too old to work. Some people work with organizations like the Audubon Society to help birds. Others concentrate their efforts on contributing time and money to organizations that are trying to preserve natural habitats. Helping animals who can't help themselves is a time honored way to do the work of a Bodhisattva and practice loving-kindness and compassion. In Tibet, it is said that these practices reverberate back, bestowing manifold blessings. Tibetan lamas teach that saving lives helps extend your own and enhances your health and vitality.

Sharon Tracy, a Buddhist who lives in New York, says that about ten years ago, she spent a weekend in Woodstock with her spiritual teacher; after she left the teacher, she was driving in a car with a friend when she spotted some poor dead creature by the side of the road. Because she had just left her teacher's presence, she said she was wide open to the experience. Suddenly she was aware of a keen sense of empathy for the suffering of all animals everywhere. For a moment, she knew what they were feeling. Sharon said that she turned to her friend, and described what she was experiencing. Her friend said, 'I'm not feeling that, and I'm glad I'm not feeling that.'

That day marked a real turning point in her life. Since then Sharon has devoted much of her time to aiding helpless animals. She has rescued countless cats and dogs and found them homes. She keeps several animals with severe physical problems in her apartment, where she cares for them. Using her own financial resources, she works to get as many of the dogs and cats she encounters spayed and neutered. Each evening, she drives around Brooklyn to deserted spots where feral cats congregate; there she leaves food. Before returning home, she drives to a cemetery where several wild dogs live in order to leave them food. There is a large dog living there whom she has been unsuccessful in capturing for more than ten years. Just last week, she was able to catch another of the dogs, a young female. This dog, whom she named Sunshine, is currently living in a veterinarian's office getting healthy enough to be placed in a permanent home.

Sharon says that in some ways, although this is not what she intended, this caretaking has become her spiritual practice. Unfortunately, it also makes it impossible for her to do other things she would like to. For example, she would like to make a pilgrimage to Nepal to study, but she can't. As she says, 'There are all these guys waiting to be fed here.'

LEARNING FROM ALL CREATURES, GREAT AND SMALL

I have a friend who declares that his relationship with his dog gives him the most perfect win/win scenario in his life. I understand because I also have a relationship with a dog, a large white sheepdog named Chandi. What joy! What love! How good for my blood pressure! Spending time with my dog is such a simple, boyish relaxed pleasure.

When we connect with the pets who consent to share our homes, not only do we feel accepted and loved, we also feel comforted and even understood. One woman recently told me that her cat has become an important part of her piano practice. Whenever she is working and concentrating on a difficult piece of music, her cat comes and sits on the piano bench with her as if to give support. A young couple I know has been going through a difficult time lately because of a stressful financial situation. They say that when they get home in the evening, playing with their two kittens is what allows them to unwind and keep from snapping at each other. Animals seem to have a definite and healing presence. They help us connect beneath the level of our own intellectual constructs. Our dog friends help us to cool out, to play, and to just take a walk; our cat friends come and sit like cosmic queens on our lap, showing us how to just be.

I realized one day that I might have gone over the top in my feelings for Chandi. I was driving to Western Massachusetts, and the dog was with me; when I looked in the rearview mirror, I could see Chandi's big serene face staring back. I was so happy. All was right with the world. *I'm driving Chandi,* I thought, *my life has meaning.* I remembered how I used to feel when my late teacher, the Dzogchen master Nyoshul Khenpo, would come from Bhutan to visit, and I would drive him around to show him the northeastern United States. My feeling of blissful contentment was very similar. In my car, driving around, being in the presence of Nyoshul Khenpo and Chandi felt so similar; I experienced the same kind of inner delight – a joyful sense of the good fortune of serving. *Am I crazy or what?* I thought to myself. *Is there no difference between my relationship with a holy Tibetan lama and my dog?* Then I realized that what I was responding to was the sense of total presence, peaceful joy, and unconditional love that Chandi emanates, and simultaneously evokes in me – not unlike what my own spiritual master evoked.

In India, when seekers make pilgrimages to revered gurus or sacred sites, they call the experience 'darshan.' 'Darshan' means viewing or entering the presence of the sacred. 'Presence' is the operative word. Nature is all about presence. When we see a great wild animal such as a lion, a tiger, an elephant, or a giraffe, even in a zoo, we are struck by its awesome presence. When we visit the Grand Canyon or a sylvan lake, we know we're in the presence of something greater than ourselves. Anyone who has ever climbed a mountain remembers what it feels like to scramble above the tree line and feel a whole new sense of grandeur, space, and freedom.

Many people say that when they are in nature, they feel closer to the sacred; they are in God's country, so to speak. I know a woman named Naomi who is an ardent nature lover and 'birder.' She says that viewing little birds through binoculars brings her a moving sense of intimacy and connectedness with nature, and hence with herself. For her birdwatching is an excellent mindfulness meditation practice. Describing this, she says, 'We walk through the world, and fortunately there are often little brown birds around us, but they seem meaningless; we're so busy we don't really notice them. Then when they are in their natural environment, and we stop and carefully watch how they move, live, and relate to each other, we can see the precious detail that the creative force bestows on every living thing.

'Looking at birds, and any animal in nature, brings us closer to our own essential self, our own purity. Puffins, for example, will sometimes fly as much as a hundred miles out to sea to get fish to feed their babies. When I see something like that, I'm touched by the innocence; I'm reminded that things in nature are simpler and more basic.'

Nature in all its forms is impressive, but it's not always filled with cute, cuddly, furry creatures. Sometimes it's just frightening; other times it can seem violent or repulsive. For some people, the unpredictable quality of the natural world is very scary. Many of us are frightened by spiders, snakes, and other creepy crawly things; some people won't take a step, no matter how well the trail is marked, because it seems so over-powering and frightening.

There is a Tibetan term, the 'drala principle,' which speaks to what we feel most deeply about nature. 'Drala' means 'beyondness' or 'beyond otherness.' 'Drala' is beyond dualism or conflict; it's so much bigger than we are that it speaks to a largeness that is beyond our full comprehension or under-standing. The spirit of nature is a good example of drala; Mother Nature is a personification of drala. When we connect to nature, or the elements of nature – fire, water, earth, air – we connect to the drala principle. When we throw a paper airplane into the air, we connect to the drala of the air. In Tibet, people write prayers on cloth flags and hang them out to flap in the breeze. In this way, they use the unseen vibrations of the drala's voices to carry their prayerful wishes into the cosmos. I was amazed the first time I saw long lines of these colorful prayer flags strung so high up on wires and ropes above perilous mountain passes; it seemed impossible that anyone could have managed to negotiate the climb that was necessary to hang them up.

Tibetans also put prayer wheels into streams to harness the power of the water element so that even while the devout are sleeping, their prayers can be going forth to bless the water, the fish, and all the other creatures. To connect to the drala by using the element of earth, many Tibetans carve mantras on stones. These 'mani stones,' as they are called, are often piled up until they become long walls of mantras. Sometimes they too are put into streams so that the mantras can be carried along on water.

When we garden or arrange flowers, we are connecting to the drala; when we walk in the woods, or swim in a natural body of water, we are connecting to the drala. These connections we make with the natural world help us heal and grow spiritually.

I always love it when I go to Hawaii to teach. The weather is always great, and I love the lush beauty of the islands, beaches, and beautiful fish. It's an awesome natural drala experience – everything from a volcano park with steam hissing out of the crater as you stand there, to snorkeling and swimming, moving like a fish among the beautiful tropical and slow moving, ancient, behemoth sea turtles.

A couple of years ago my friend Barbara, founder of the Buddhist Peace Park on the Big Island, suggested that I go with her to do a little exploring of the islands. We took her grandson Blake, who was about six at the time, and we went to the southernmost tip of the Hawaiian chain. We drove as far as we could and then left the car and walked over the sharp volcanic rock at the edge of the shore – all the way out to the tippy-tip of the Big Island, the last piece of land sticking out to the south in the vast Pacific Ocean. It is a remarkable site, a real power point. There, we sat down on little foam rubber cushions.

The ground there is covered with lava rock; I remember looking down and being amazed at the way the hot lava from a nearby volcano had spilled over, flowed down, and hardened in place to form the ground at the edge of the sea. I had the feeling that we were sitting out in the middle of the infinite blue Pacific. On that point, water crashes and rushes in from both east and west. It felt windy and wild even though the temperature was still warm and balmy. I was overwhelmed by the sense of nature's power and exquisitely aware of the energy of the infinite sea, sky, wind, volcano, and the igneous rock beneath us.

Little Blake was excitedly scampering around like a mountain goat – and not without our becoming concerned and anxious, I might add. We tried to get him to simply sit with us for a bit and take in the view, but he wanted to run around.

Finally, Blake said, 'Lama, can we call the local gods?'

I said, 'Why not?' Who was I to know more than a local boy?

So we did some chants together, and I performed some 'mudras' – hand gestures of invocation and prayerful communication. Suddenly, as though on cue, a school of dolphins appeared, powerfully arching and cresting above the waves. I was impressed to say the least. I would have to say, however, that although Blake loved the spectacle, he took it in stride.

For a moment, we all felt as though we had indeed been able to summon the local deities in the form of creatures of the sea; I think we all felt deeply connected to the free-spirited creatures, who jumped and dived for our benefit. When the wave crests turned into leaping silver schools of dolphins, it was as if Mother Nature's face miraculously appeared where before there was nothing but sky. This was like encountering the drala face to face. I have never forgotten it. Now, whenever I make prayers and mudra gestures, I still see those silver seraphs swimming before me.

The invisible infinite has to take form in some way so that we can relate to it. Perhaps this is how the invisible formless, most high, manifests in Hawaii. If we were in the Amazon, it might be the jaguar. In the Rockies, it might be the golden eagle; in the Delaware Water Gap it might be a red hawk and in the Himalayas, a snow leopard, or even a yeti.

Most of us have experienced times when we have been able to lose ourselves in the power and wonder of nature. You don't have to go to the Hawaiian Islands to feel connected to nature and feel the intense energy of the universe. There may even be such a place in your own neighborhood. I know for certain that there is a place within you.

Sometimes you have to make a little effort to connect to nature, but it's always worth it. I'm often shocked when I'm on public beaches early in the morning or after six on a summer evening. Typically the crowds are gone, and one is much more conscious of the primordially wild beauty of the sea and sand. If I'm in Martha's Vineyard in the summer, I sometimes go down to Menemsha Bay to watch the sunset. There, the beach is always filled with people, and as the sun goes down, everyone bows westward, cheers, and positively loses his or her sense of propriety; for a brief moment, even the adults become like kids again. Being with a bunch of people who are uninhibitedly cheering the sun is a great experience.

Nature is healing; its silence is comforting and soothing. Nature can also help heal our relationships. Try taking a walk in the woods with a friend or romantic partner. Bring along a little picnic lunch or at least something to drink. Notice your surroundings, pay close attention to the sounds and the movements of the birds and other little creatures. See how much simpler things appear, and how much easier it is to connect with each other. Try spending a specific portion of a day together in nature practicing Noble Silence as a way of opening to deeper forms of communications.

Today more than ever, we see that no one is able to be entirely isolated. We are all citizens of planet earth. What we do today influences the ozone layer, the rain forest, the children, and the future. We all need to develop greater vision and deeper ecological understanding. Let's save the planet for our children as well as the whales.

IMPROVE YOUR KARMA AND EARTH'S KARMA – OUTER PRACTICES

I recently saw an advertisement that Home Depot had placed in a newspaper. It announced that the chain of superstores had adopted an environmental wood purchasing practice and had committed itself to stop selling products made from the trees in old growth forests in environmentally sensitive areas. The ad said that Home Depot considered the cutting down of such trees barbaric. I thought 'barbaric' was an interesting and appropriate choice of words. Obviously

Home Depot has realized that it is wise to protect the trees and the forests, and that it will ultimately prove to be good business as well as good sense. The entire fragile ecosystem is our home, after all. It will be hard to replace or even just replenish it.

It's incumbent on all of us to try to find ways of approaching our home planet with greater respect and less barbaric attitudes. We have to start somewhere, no matter how small our actions may appear to be. I'm sure we all have our own list of things that we can do to help the earth and its inhabitants. Here are some suggestions (feel free to add your own):

✳ Plant a tree, a garden, or even a few plants.

✳ Conserve water.

✳ Don't use a car when it's not necessary; become accustomed to walking or riding a bicycle at least some of the time.

✳ Find less toxic ways to handle insect infestations. (I'm told that ants, for example, are repelled by bay leaves.)

✳ Don't kill any creature unnecessarily.

✳ Try to avoid buying or using products that harm any beings, either in their production or application.

✳ Recycle bottles, cans, plastics, and paper.

✳ Find alternatives to wearing fur.

✳ Eat less meat (even if you don't want to become a vegetarian, cutting back on meat consumption can make a difference).

✳ Cut back on fish as a meat substitute. (The seas also need our help.)

✳ Become more aware of practices that are damaging animals and may ultimately harm us as well (the use of hormones in farming, and the cruel slaughter of ducks to provide feathers and down, for example).

✳ Purchase nontoxic cleaning agents. Try using vinegar and baking soda to clean, and Bon Ami to scrub.

✳ Conserve electricity.

✳ Be aware of the suffering of laboratory animals and petition universities, drug companies, and research centers to look for wiser ways.

✳ Try to buy organic fruits and vegetables to reduce the use of pesticides.

✳ Become aware of the ways that certain kinds of factory farming and genetic engineering of food can harm the environment, and incorporate that information into your purchasing.

MEDITATING THROUGH THE SEASONS – INNER PRACTICE

Almost thirty years ago, after my first trip to India, my girlfriend Tina and I spent a summer living in semi-retreat in a national forest on the slopes of Mount Shasta in northern California. We had a tent, but since it never seemed to rain, we used it mainly to store things, while we slept outside. From the high slopes where we sat, we could see both sunrise and sunset, so we meditated every morning at dawn and every evening as it gradually grew dark.

I remember one morning I was off by myself, sitting under a tree, wrapped in a maroon woolen cape that Tina had made for me. I was sitting in meditation with my eyes closed, following the breath at my nostrils instead of poking my nose into anyone else's business; I was just enjoying the glorious morning moment. But then I felt a gentle touch nibbling at my left shoulder. Like a good meditator, I kept my eyes closed, and let it be. I wondered what it was. Maybe a mosquito? My mind became even quieter. Then again I noticed that the touch at my shoulder had grown slightly more insistent, turning into a veritable tug. Very quietly and slowly, I turned my head, opened my eyes, and discovered that I was staring straight into the beautiful eyes of a large doe. What was this? Maybe it was my animal ally or totem. Maybe it was a friend from another life and another mountain. We shared a moment locked in each other's gaze. Neither of us were scared or startled. It was absolutely lovely. Then the deer slowly straightened up and trotted gracefully into the deep woods. Was this a dream? This special visitation blessed my whole day – my whole week. I felt as if I had sat with the local gods. I can still see those brown doe eyes.

The great Tibetan yogi, Milarepa, lived his entire life outdoors, meditating on the mountains and in the many caves in the Tibetan countryside. 'Nature,' he sang in one of his spontaneous songs, 'is the only book I need to read.'

Meditating in nature is a beautiful way to make us more aware of the connection between our own Buddha-ness, our Buddha-nature, and nature as a whole. The Buddha meditated in the forest and along the roadside. As we know, he realized perfect enlightenment while sitting under a tree. Here are four ideas for seasonal meditations to help you on your own path of awakening.

SPRING – FLOWER MEDITATION

Most of us have seen photographs of cherry blossom season in Japan. When I lived there, I discovered that plum blossoms arrive even earlier, usually in February, as a signal that winter does not last forever. Several times in this country, I've been in Washington, D.C., just in time to see cherry blossoms herald another spring. What good luck!

Spring is a time of rebirth. We can welcome it in by praying and meditating in a garden that is beginning to bud. In New England, I sometimes see the little purple crocuses pushing through while there is still snow on the ground. Then come the daffodils, finally the tulips. What blooms first in the gardens in your part of the world?

Spring is an appropriate time to do a mindfulness meditation centered on flower arranging. In Japan, the Zen art of flower arranging is known as 'Kado' – the Way (or Path) of Flowers, or 'ikebana,' which translates as pond flower. Literally speaking, when we practice Kado, we should let go of the Western notion of 'arranging.' Rather, we should approach the flowers in a meditative state of mind so that they reveal their own nature. Then we won't have to arrange them according to any preconceived pattern, but can 'feel' how they want and wish to be placed.

The flowers that you choose to arrange in the spring will, of course, depend on where you live. Here in the Northeast, we have apple blossoms, cherry blossoms, pussy willows, and mountain laurel, to name just a few. Of course if you don't have access to flowers in their natural habitat, you can choose any kind of flower or greenery from a florist. Whatever flowers you decide on, the idea is to work with them mindfully and reverently. Flower arranging is like making a sacred altar.

Stay in the immediacy of the present moment, and choose

your blossoms carefully one by one. Look at the flower or piece of greenery. Get a feeling of where it was grown, and how it blossomed. Cut off the bottom of the stems individually – carefully, attentively, lovingly. Find a container, whether it be a crystal vase, a ceramic bowl, or a simple metal pot, that suits the blossoms. Put water in the vase. Arrange your flowers carefully, one by one. Remain in the moment, and don't rush. In Japan, flowers are often placed asymmetrically in order to achieve a fully three-dimensional effect. Sometimes a flower is so heartbreakingly beautiful that it seems meant to be in a vase alone.

When you are finished, place your flowers somewhere where they can be viewed. If you have an altar, you might want to place them there. See if you can find a spot where the flowers can become the focal point.

When I first stayed in a Buddhist monastery in Bodh Gaya, we were encouraged not to throw out the blossoms when they began to droop. Instead it was suggested that we let the flowers wilt and die, one by one; we would observe the petals falling and then meditate on the transient beauty and impermanence of all that lives.

SUMMER – WATER-GAZING MEDITATION

Ramakrishna was a great nineteenth-century Hindu spiritual teacher in Bengal. As a young man, he practiced different disciplines including Islam and Christianity. Because of his intense mystical and spiritual experiences, he was able to see and recognize the validity and connectedness of all spiritual traditions.

One of the things that I always remember about Ramakrishna's teachings is that he told his followers that whenever they saw water, they should meditate. What did he mean by that? Did he mean that we should sit cross-legged every time we turn on the faucet or even see falling rain? It's a funny image, but I don't think that's what he meant. I think he meant that we can use water to remind ourselves of the inner lake of peace or the flowing nature of all things. Water – whether it be a waterfall, the ocean's waves, a puddle, a swimming pool, a puddle, a raindrop, or even a teardrop – reflects back on the pure, crystalline, refreshing nature of inner spirit. Water represents the innate clarity of mind; it soothes and quenches the soul.

In the summer, I love to meditate by the side of a body of water, whether it be a lake, a stream, or the ocean. But you can do it anywhere. Even a fish tank will do. Not everyone is fortunate enough to live or work near a body of pure, clean water, but I'm always astonished at how many large cities have fountains and fishponds in unlikely places. Even midtown Manhattan has a pocket park in the East 50s with an ersatz, but very satisfying, waterfall. My brilliant copy editor tells me that her sister-in-law meditated there when she was in labor.

Sit by water.
Count your breaths as if they are waves.
In breath . . . One
Out breath . . . Two
In breath . . . Three
Let the regular wavelike motion of the breath
wash away all your cares.
Let it carry you home.
Float on the breath of the present moment.
Let the water meditate for you.
Flow with it.

✳

FALL – AN ANALYTICAL MEDITATION

When many people think of meditation, they seem to think primarily of meditations that involve resting the mind. Yet there is another kind of meditation that involves using the intellect and discriminating faculties of the mind to analyze reality.

The season of fall represents passage and the beautiful poignancy and transitory nature of life itself. What better time to use meditation and the powers of your mind to contemplate the laws of karma – cause and effect – in your own life?

Start with today. Look at how your day progressed from beginning to end. Be very detail-oriented and specific. Consider the particular events that occurred. What went wrong? What went right? Can you see how karma unfolded? Take your time. Apply your best analytical thinking to it.

You can use this technique to analyze anything. Pick your subject and maintain it. Contemplate an important relationship in your life. What have you done to create the relationship that exists? How about the last week, month, or year of your life? Sometimes it's very easy to see the interwoven karmic connections; other times it takes work and effort. Don't back away from this analytical meditation if you become unhappy with what you are seeing. Remember this kind of meditation is a way to gain greater awareness into the nature of reality — what is — in your life and in general. Try to directly perceive and comprehend the effects of karma.

WINTER – WALKING MEDITATION

Connect to the experience of winter with a walking meditation. All you need is some comfortable clothing and a place where you can walk undisturbed for twenty or thirty minutes — even if it's back and forth in your yard or on your block. Take the dog if you have one. I always do. The minute I reach for my hooded parka, Chandi runs to the door.

If there is snow on the ground, it can be fun to walk where it crunches under your feet. Many people, myself included, like walking on beaches and boardwalks in winter weather. If you live in warmer climates, these can be good places for walking in the cooler temperatures of winter.

The path is right beneath your feet
Make a conscious step on it.
Then another. And now another.
Count your steps.
Right footstep . . . count one.
Left foot . . . count two.
Right foot . . . three.
Left foot . . . four.
Walking along the path to enlightenment . . .
Connecting with yourself
by just doing what you are doing, one hundred percent.
One step at a time.

CHAPTER EIGHT

Joyfully Crazy and Wonderful Awakenings

I did toy with the idea of doing a cook-book . . . The recipes were to be the routine ones: how to make dry toast, instant coffee, hearts of lettuce and brownies. But as an added attraction, at no extra charge, my idea was to put a fried egg on the cover. I think a lot of people who hate literature but love fried eggs would buy it if the price was right.

– Groucho Marx

There is so much joyous wisdom in humor, isn't there? Laughing has its own uplifting energy, which can become even more spiritual when it's shared. As seekers, can we find the wisdom buried in this silly Groucho Marx quote? It's funny, it's ironic, and it's absurd. Just like life!

Recently I was on a beach in Brooklyn, New York, with a friend of mine. We were sitting on our towels like beached Buddhas staring out at the water, over our sunburnt bellies. To our right was a long, impressive jetty made of rocks stretching out into the water. Suddenly a human form appeared unexpectedly around the jetty, at first swimming horizontally across the horizon and then into shore. It was a large, older man in a skimpy red bathing suit wearing a black-and-white polka dot shower cap – not a bathing cap – on his head. When he reached shore, he carefully picked a spot and laid down on the sand. But he wasn't finished with his routine. He proceeded to roll around and around, shimmying up and down on the sand, resembling a huge, amiable brown bear scratching himself on a large oak tree. He looked like he was having a whale of a great time. I should add that as outlandish as his behavior appeared, he also seemed quite sane and composed, as well as completely un-self-conscious. He was clearly doing this for some purpose. (Aren't we all usually doing things for a purpose?) When he was covered with sand, head to toe – even his shower cap – he plunged back into the water and swam back around the jetty and away.

What was he doing? Was this just one scene of some bet he was trying to win, or a self-imposed task he'd dreamed up for himself while under the influence? My friend and I decided that most likely this was some health regimen that he had worked out for himself. It seemed to be working, for he was obviously a strong, physically fit man. *What*, I asked myself, *could we all learn from watching his routine?*

For me, a lesson emerged from this man's complete lack of self-consciousness. It was positively liberating to see him doing his thing, totally immersed in his own absurd antics. Watching him was a little like being entertained by a clown – at the circus, on television, or even on a street corner. When clowns frolic, and juggle, and mime, don't they also appear completely unself-conscious? But clown–like performers are acting for the benefit of their audiences. The swimmer on the Brooklyn beach was genuinely unself-conscious. He was doing what he was doing with complete focus, for his own benefit, whatever that might be. When he plopped himself on the sand, a few feet away from our towels, he knew that people would look at him. Short of covering our eyes, we had no choice. Yet he didn't care if people found his antics incomprehensible. This guy was totally oblivious; it was as if the beach were deserted.

In Tibet there is a spiritual tradition that is seen as having a connection with such incomprehensible behavior. Known as 'crazy wisdom,' it is embodied by enlightened vagabonds and an entire lineage of male yogis and female yoginis who throughout the centuries have behaved in ways that people didn't always understand. Some of these masters, for example, spent their lives meditating in mountaintop aeries like eagles, descending into valley villages only occasionally for alms, as bedraggled as wild animals. There are stories of Tibetan masters who vowed never to sleep indoors; masters who rarely, if ever, slept or wore clothes, even in the frigid Himalayas; masters who answered whatever they were asked by repeating exactly what was said to them. A student might question such a master saying, 'How are you today, holy teacher?' and his teacher's response would be, 'How are you today, holy teacher?' Such a master would often do this no matter what the question. 'How are you today, crazy wastrel?' would be answered in kind: 'How are you today, crazy wastrel?' Among Tibetans, teaching tales abound, even today, about some of these most colorful and unique spiritual practitioners.

The salient point to remember here is the wisdom, not just the craziness, for spiritual teachings lead us to a higher form of sanity. The 'crazy wisdom' of Tibetan masters reveals a heightened form of lucidity that is able to cut through the superficial layers of social convention and customs. It is based on brilliant insight into how things actually are, as opposed to how they appear. Crazy wisdom shows a direct, raw appreciation for life as well as a cosmic sense of humor. It is what the Sufi author Idries Shah has dubbed 'the wisdom of the idiots.'

Tibet's inspired upholders of crazy wisdom have typically disdained speculative metaphysics and institutionalized religious forms in favor of a style that can loosely be described as 'letting it all hang out.' These divine madmen prefer to celebrate the unconditional freedom of enlightenment through divinely inspired foolishness. Their frequent refusal to pay homage to external religious forms and moral systems reminds us of the inherent freedom and sacredness that can be found in authentic being. This freedom often extends beyond conventional piety and morality. An enlightened Tibetan meditation master of old, Choying Rangdrol, spent his life in meditation on a floor mat, wearing only a loose sheepskin coat. He said, 'Yogis want and need nothing other than the immutable nature of authentic being.' Milarepa, Tibet's enlightened poet, once sang, 'My lineage is crazy: crazed by devotion, crazed by truth, crazy about Dharma.'

One of my favorite crazy wisdom stories is about an Indian tantric adept named Saraha, who lived in the third century. It was often the custom in India at that time for fearlessly unorthodox yogis to form relationships with women from lower castes. In this way, they helped demonstrate the possibility of freedom from concepts, such as the rigid caste system. When Saraha, who was already considered mad, went off to the jungle with a lower caste teenage servant girl, village tongues wagged.

Saraha's consort, who genuinely admired the crazy-wise master, told him that he could persevere in his meditation and yogic practices, while she would take care of daily chores and necessities. Saraha was so intensely engaged with meditation that he rarely showed any interest in food, other than to eat what was placed in front of him. One day, however, he suddenly made a strange request. 'Bring me radish curry!' he said.

The young woman took great time and care to prepare the curry exactly as she thought Saraha would wish. After busying herself in food preparation, she finally brought him a plate of woven leaves, upon which was placed a generous portion of curry and some buffalo milk yogurt. Placing it in front of him she noticed that Saraha was in deep meditation, travelling to places she could not imagine. So she left him sitting there.

Twelve years passed, and Saraha did not move. All the while, the young woman stayed with him.

Suddenly, Rip Van Winkle fashion, Saraha stood up. 'Where,' he asked, 'is the radish curry I requested?'

Saraha's consort was astonished. 'Crazy master,' she said. 'The radish season has come and gone many times. For twelve long years, you've sat in meditation, like a radish yourself – silently stuck in the earth. Now you still want curry? You call this meditation – holding onto a radish all these years!' Thus she awakened him.

And then the young woman, like the true dakini she really was, proved her own capacity for insightful wisdom. 'Sitting cross-legged,' she said, 'that's not true meditation. Living isolated away from family and friends, that's not genuine solitude. Authentic solitude means parting from discursive thoughts and dualistic concepts. But you've spent twelve years sitting, mentally holding an illusory radish! What kind of yogi are you anyway?'

It is said that due to the clarity of her insight, Yogi Saraha was immediately enlightened.

The pioneering Tibetan lama, Chogyam Trungpa Rinpoche, once described crazy wisdom as an innocent state of mind that has the quality of early morning – fresh, sparkling, and completely awake. He also described the principle of crazy wisdom as the starting point for an exciting spiritual journey, not just as its fruit.

The great Chogyam Trungpa was no stranger to crazy wisdom. There is an often told story about the day back in the 1970s, when the wandering American seeker and holy man Bhagwan Das was visiting Trungpa in Boulder. Trungpa was well known for his capacity to handle liquor; he and

Bhagwan sat down together for a drink one night. And Trungpa promptly began literally to drink Bhagwan Das under the table. As the evening progressed, Bhagwan Das became so blotto that he didn't know or care what happened next. Trungpa took this opportunity to free Bhagwan Das from what some thought might perhaps be his greatest attachment – his long, matted, holy man beard and longer hair. When Bhagwan woke up the next morning, shorn like a sheep, he was furious. But what could he do? The crazy wisdom master, his teaching completed, was gone, and Bhagwan Das was left to deal with his own feelings and to take what he could from the irascible Tibetan master's teaching.

HOLY FOLLY

Buddhism isn't alone in its reverence for holy fools and the pure state of mind that they represent. Throughout the centuries, across the world, the archetype of the holy fool has been identified with the spiritual quest and the search for truth and meaning. The Greek and Russian Orthodox religions, for example, both have a tradition of 'holy folly.' In the Byzantine tradition, pilgrims, monks, and other seekers sometimes took eccentricity to the brink of madness and beyond. Like the Tibetan holy men, many practiced extreme asceticism, travelling nearly naked in the dead of winter, frequently casting off socially acceptable behavior along with their clothing. They were giving it all to God and leaving it all up to God, as it were, in unimaginable acts of self-sacrifice and renunciation.

A well-known Anglo Saxon heroic legend concerns the search for the Holy Grail and the Arthurian knight, Percival (Parcifal), whose very name means innocent fool. As the story evolves, the young and naive Percival leaves his home and, through a series of chance happenings, encounters several knights from King Arthur's court, and finally meets King Arthur himself. At first, there is no way that Percival would have been considered 'knight material.' However, as much because of his innocent belief as anything else, Percival is able to shock everyone by conquering the formidable Red Knight. In so doing, Percival becomes a knight.

As a knight, Percival's primary quest is to find the Holy Grail, the chalice that Jesus Christ is said to have used when sharing the Last Supper with his disciples. Percival's search takes him to the castle of the Fisher King, a wounded leader living within a wasted land that reflects the king's depressed and crippled state. The legend within the Grail Kingdom is that the king can be healed and his kingdom restored if a completely pure and innocent fool enters the kingdom and asks the right question. Then and only then will the king be healed and the Holy Grail be found. Percival, of course, is the holy fool. But even Percival's childlike innocence and pure view of the world has been distorted, for he has been socialized and taught by others not to ask questions. So even though the holy fool, Percival, frames a question in his heart and mind, he fails to ask it, and thus fails to heal the king.

Many of us today walk around with too many answers. The

right question, of course, can often be the key that unlocks the universe.

CONNECTING TO YOUR OWN HOLY FOOL

Within each of us there is a holy fool, the soul who is staring out at a spiritual quest with eyes filled with wonder and awe. This is the incorruptible, eternal inner child who symbolizes trust, innocence, and purity. We all started our lives as holy fools, but for most of us it takes spiritual effort to stay connected to the little Buddha within. Still, we can reawaken that little Buddha at any age.

Friends who know such things tell me that in the tarot deck, the card for the Fool symbolizes the beginning of a journey of adventure and discovery. No one can begin a journey of discovery without tapping into the holy fool within. We can't move forward unless we access our innate purity and see the world afresh with the innocence of a child. As adults too often our vision is obscured by our jaded preconceptions and projections, which act like veils over our eyes.

We all know the story of the emperor who needs a new wardrobe and hears about an exceptionally gifted tailor. When the emperor visits the tailor he is suitably impressed by what the tailor tells him and orders a new set of the clothing, which is to be the most expensive and magnificent in the world. On the day the clothing arrives, with great fanfare the tailor opens a box, which is totally empty, and helps the emperor try on the fantasy clothing. 'Look,' the tailor says, pointing to air. 'Notice the fine rubies on the lapels.' First the emperor, buck naked, parades around his palace while his entire court oohs and aahs. Finally the emperor walks down the street so his people can admire his finery. The people clap; they shout their approval. 'Look at the emperor!' They scream, 'Doesn't he look beautiful in his amazing clothing?' Finally in the back of the crowd, the small voice of a child is heard. 'But mommy,' the child says, 'the emperor is naked.'

The fool is the child who knows instinctively when the emperor is naked, no matter what he is being told by society. He's not burdened by concepts or preconceived ideas about reality. He sees what is, and he's free to take chances. The fool is free to say what's on his mind. Medieval courts frequently had a fool or jester, who was one of the only people free to speak his mind to the sovereign and still keep his head.

Most of us are quite removed from such profound freedom; we are so layered and encrusted with socialized attitudes that we can't loosen up our habitualized inhibitions and canned opinions. We have so much invested in achieving a certain status, in being part of things, in fitting into the prevailing zeitgeist and its mores and values. We worry about appearances, image, and what people will think of us. We see mostly what we have been taught to see. We like the movies, books, art, theater, and dance that critics tell us to like. We eat at restaurants that have received good reviews and word of mouth. We admire the people who we are told have celebrity or status. Sometimes, in fact, it feels as though all of life is filtered through someone else's opinions. We sample everything through someone else's eyes before we experience or feel it for ourselves. Much of this comes from having been monitored and given feedback from our parents. This is a developmental issue from early childhood. Later we struggle for acceptance from our peers, and soon after from people who hold our romantic interest. Every generation has its own ideas about what is acceptable behavior, even when rebelling and being nonconformist. Many kids today pierce their navels and various body parts. In my time it was the hair thing – beards, moustaches, sideburns, and long hair.

Crazy wisdom consistently reminds us to feel what we truly feel; it reminds us to stay in touch with our own inner values. It reminds us to be genuine and sensitive – to stay in touch with the open-eyed fool within, the childlike inner soul unencumbered by socialization and convention.

The Dharma encourages us to learn to look at things with fresh vision, as if for the first time. That's why Trungpa Rinpoche, the great crazy wisdom master, titled his collection of poetry *First Thought, Best Thought*. The little Buddhas within us all have untarnished eyes, capable of seeing truth. If we can access that perspective we will bring balance and joy to our lives instead of always taking a rational and cerebral approach. We can tap into an inexhaustible inner well of spontaneous delight.

A story: Not that long ago, Dave was having lunch with some friends in a restaurant where he often eats. He ordered a bowl of chicken soup. When it came, Dave looked down and saw that he had no spoon. He laughed and he began to tell his friends a joke he had heard about a wise and learned Eastern European rabbi of old. It seems that this rabbi believed in the wisdom we can attain through personal experience, and preferred to teach by showing rather than telling. One day the rabbi and his wife walked into his favorite restaurant and ordered his favorite meal, mushroom barley soup. The waiter put the soup down in front of the rabbi and went back to the kitchen. The rabbi was very hungry and wanted to eat, but when he looked down, he realized the waiter had failed to give him a spoon. *Ah, an opportunity for a lesson.* He waited patiently until the waiter appeared again, and when he did, he said, 'My friend, would you please taste this soup?'

The waiter said, 'Oh, I'm very busy right now. I don't have time to taste soup. Besides my boss would be furious if he saw me eating my customer's food.'

'Please,' the rabbi said, 'I beg of you. I just want you to taste this soup. If anyone says anything, I will explain. Do this as a favor to me.'

The waiter sighed, put down his tray, and went over to taste the soup. When he looked down, he realized what the rabbi was asking. Laughing, the waiter brought the rabbi a spoon.

Dave looked at his friends, and suggested they try it with the waitress. 'Helen,' he said to her, 'come here and taste this soup.'

'Oh Dave,' Helen replied, 'I don't have the time to taste your soup. I'm busy. What's wrong with the soup?'

'Nothing's wrong with the soup,' Dave continued. 'I just want you to taste it.'

'Puh-lease . . .' Helen moaned. 'Don't I look busy enough for you?'

'Come on. One little taste,' Dave pleaded.

'Oh all right,' Helen said. She came over and looked down at the table. 'Oh,' she said, 'you have no spoon.' Having said that, she shrugged, picked up the bowl in her hands and took a sip. 'It tastes good to me,' she said, as she walked away to wait on another customer.

The question, of course, is who is wise, and who is foolish?

In his seminal book on this subject, appropriately entitled *Crazy Wisdom,* Wes Nisker writes:

'Crazy wisdom is the wisdom of the saint, the Zen master, the poet, the mad scientist, and the fool. Crazy wisdom sees that we live in a world of many illusions, that the Emperor has no clothes, and that much of human belief and behavior is ritualized nonsense. Crazy wisdom understands anti-matter and old Sufi poetry; loves paradox and puns and pie fights and laughing at politicians. Crazy wisdom flips the world upside down and backward until everything becomes perfectly clear.'

FOOLISH CHOICES

Recently I talked to a woman who was going through a particularly messy divorce. 'I should have known,' she said. 'In fact, I did know. I just didn't pay attention to what I knew.' She went on to talk more about her husband, saying, 'He seemed to fit the bill of the kind of man I should marry. He was successful, he was attractive, he was well educated. He had all the superficial characteristics of the kind of man I was expected to marry. But as it turns out we never really had anything in common.'

Listening to this woman reminded me that sometimes when we make important decisions and choices in life, we need to consult with our own inner, and holy, fool. We need to look at our choices with a fresh eye, and ask ourselves whether we are moving in a direction that brings us closer or further away from truth, from enlightenment. We need to be certain that we are not simply trying to conform to somebody else's cookie cutter version of what life should be. Sometimes the wisest action we can take is the one that appears most bizarre and least practical to everyone around us. And yet often we feel as if all our choices are defined by what others expect.

When I went off to India right after college graduation, everyone thought I was crazy. Then, when I didn't return to America for years and years, they were quite sure of it. My dad used to say that he didn't understand how I could live for so many years 'without even a pot to piss in,' as he so pungently put it. The surprising sense and internal logic of my personal spiritual journey was not evident to my family and friends; I must admit that it wasn't really clear to me either at the time.

Of course it is always so much easier for all of us to apply twenty-twenty hindsight and thus discern deeper, unseen patterns and higher purposes not too obvious to the naked eye in the present moment. Looking back now, I can trace my post-college trajectory through Asia and back to the West almost as if it had been scripted, and I was only following the plotline. Then, everyone thought I was crazy; now it makes perfect sense. My mother says that it took her and my late dad 'decades to get used to it.' That is how outlandish and non-sensical they thought my path was. But eventually they too came to see it all differently.

Now I often remind my mother that family tradition helped shape my behavior. When I was a child, my parents, my brother, my sister, and I used to take family vacations that were essentially road trips. I fondly remember driving down to Florida along the east coast, for example – three kids in the back seat of a large 1956 DeSoto with a push-button auto-matic transmission and a V-8 engine. Sometimes at night, my parents would stop at a drive-in movie. My mother would fit out the back seat with pillows so that we could watch the movie until we fell asleep. One of us little kids would sleep on the back window shelf, one on the back seat, and the third on the floor.

My father had a remarkable sense of direction. Even in unfamiliar states in strange places he had never been, he seemed able to give directions to others. My mother had a slightly different approach. She would say, 'Harold, let's go there,' pointing to a spot on a map. My mother – whose name is Joyce – would have no idea of whether or not the place was on the way to where we were going. She never asked, 'Is it on the way?' Instead she would say, 'I don't know. It looks like it might be good. Let's take a chance.' My father would often jokingly call her 'Take-a-Chance Joyce.' He would make a mock motion of sharply turning the wheel, and mimic the sound of screeching tires like in a cartoon, as if we were suddenly turning completely around and heading off in an entirely new direction. But often he followed her whims. Why not? It was a vacation. Thanks to this attitude, we saw all kinds of things that weren't on the AAA roadmap. We ate in unusual places, slept in motels that weren't on anybody's recommended list, and camped in sites that would never make any campgrounds of America guide. It was always fun.

I remember till this day a farmer we met near the Finger Lakes in upstate New York, and somewhere my mother still has some shaky 8-millimeter home movie footage of this kind man, Farmer Brown, putting me up onto his horse on the edge of his pasture. In the early fifties, it was one of Take-a-Chance Joyce's off road magical detours. What a wonderful adventure! I am wearing my first pair of shoes in that film.

My parents taught me to enjoy the freedom of approaching many experiences in life from an open point of view. They taught me that we can't always follow the tourist buses. We need to give ourselves permission to find our own way, whether it seems sensible or not. If we would genuinely find and follow what Thoreau referred to as a different drummer then we must be prepared to 'step to a different beat,' regardless of what society's conventions might say. There is wisdom in listening to our hearts and opening ourselves up to surprise, and the magic and mystery of life. In a world gone mad, being different enough to be regarded as crazy certainly has some virtues.

CRAZY WISDOM PRACTICE?

In a bizarre piece of synchronicity, as I was writing this, someone sent me an e-mail entitled 'Elevator Antics.' It smacks of crazy wisdom behavior so I'm including some of the suggestions. I wouldn't want to be mistaken for Serious Das, the serious author!

Things to Do on an Elevator

1. Crack open your briefcase or purse, and while peering inside, ask, 'Got enough air in there?'

2. Meow occasionally.

3. Wear a puppet on one of your hands and use it to talk to the other passengers.

4. Listen to the elevator walls with a stethoscope.

5. Say 'ding' at each floor.

6. Make noises like an explosion every time someone presses a button.

7. Stare, grinning at a friendly looking passenger, and then announce, 'I have on new socks.'

8. When the elevator is silent, look around and ask, 'Is that your beeper?'

9. Greet everyone getting on the elevator with a warm handshake and ask each of them to call you 'Admiral.'

10. Hand out lollipops or sticks of gum to your fellow passengers.

Of course, I realize that none of us are going to follow these elevator instructions. But for just a few minutes, think about doing any one of them, and imagine what it would mean to be free of your inhibitions about appearing different or foolish. Visualize yourself as somebody who isn't afraid of being laughed at. What freedom it must be to be able to stop worrying about what people think!

The purpose of crazy wisdom is to help burst the bubble of our fixed opinions and expectations. As we go through the day, isn't it often the unexpected thing that happens that perks us up and gives us something different to enthuse about when we get home? We can live on the brink of the mystery of being by bringing a bit more whimsy and playfulness to our serious deliberations.

LOSING MENTAL CONSTRUCTS

When I was in Asia, several teachers told me the same story about a renowned scholar monk in ancient China. He was a teacher, and he would go from monastery to monastery carrying the weighty tomes of written sutras, Dharma teachings, and his own lectures in bags on his back along trails up and down the mountains. Needless to say, he would get very tired. One day as he was walking up a mountain path, he came upon a tiny tea shack in which an elderly woman sold tea, noodles, and rice to pilgrims and travellers.

Now over the years, the monk had received many compliments on his erudition and knowledge, and he took himself much too seriously; in fact he had become quite haughty and conceited. On this particular day, when the monk approached the tea shack, he put down all the written manuscripts that contained his lifetime of commentaries on the wisdom scriptures and asked the old woman for some tea.

'Certainly,' she said, 'but since you are such a learned teacher, before we have tea, we must have some Dharma.'

'All of my Dharma is over there,' the monk said, pointing to the many manuscripts. 'Can you read, illiterate old lady?'

'What good is it if your Dharma is over there, outside of yourself?' the woman replied. 'What a burden that must be.'

At that moment, the monk awoke to his arrogance, realizing that carrying around all this weight was not upholding the Dharma. Instantaneously, he awoke to the fact that all the Dharma was inside himself. With tears in his eyes, he bowed to the old woman three times, saying, 'I don't need my commentaries on the scriptures any more. I'm free of that heavy burden. Thank you for pointing directly to the Dharma within me. I will leave them here for you to use as firewood.'

And the woman said, 'Now we can have our tea.'

Like the holy fool, the elderly woman along the roadside reminds us that innate truth and reality function as counterpoints to those who are still burdened with the weight of concepts and accumulated knowledge.

This is the difference between mere intellectual knowledge and spiritual realization. That is why Lao Tzu's wise *Tao Te Ching* says, 'In pursuit of the world, one gains more and more. But in pursuit of the Way one gains less and less. Loss upon loss, until at last comes rest. When nothing is undertaken, nothing remains undone.'

The message is: No appointments, no disappointments.

A WISE FOOL'S MEDITATION

Let yourself go.
Totally.
Breathe in and out a few times deeply.
Drop your body, drop your persona.
Let your hair down, and let it all hang out.
Drop your mind.
Unscrew your head
and shoot it – swoosh – through the nearest hoop
(a wastebasket will do).
Take the path of least resistance,
the lazy man's way to enlightenment.
Unedit yourself.

Let the uncontrived little Buddha inside wake up
And laugh, dance, sing, and shine.

No one is watching.
It don't matter how it looks.
Go for it!
Push the envelope of sanity.
Make the leap into irrationality.
Plumb the dark side of the moon,
the far side
of the brain —
the secret side of your mysterious primordial
Being.
Become a spiritual astronaut
a Way-farer
Unfurl your heart's wings
Breathe
Dance, laugh, play
Clap your hands
Soar
Sing

CHAPTER NINE

Spiritual Alchemy —
Embracing Life's Lessons

If you know what it means to be out in the middle of an ocean by yourself, in the dark, scared, then it gives you a feel for what every other human being is going through. I row an actual ocean. Other people have just as many obstacles to go through.

— Toni Murden, First woman to row solo
across the Atlantic Ocean

Obstacles and challenges! Life is full of them, isn't it? Sometimes it seems as though the most difficult spiritual challenge we have to meet is figuring out the connection between the challenges on our paths and the spiritual lessons we need to learn. Let's, for example, take a look at what Lois, a thirty-six-year-old designer, is experiencing right now. Lois feels as though the last two years of her life have been total hell. The first thing that happened was that her father had two heart attacks and open heart surgery. For a while, it looked as though he was going to get better, but just when he seemed to be recovering, he caught pneumonia and died. Lois, who was very close to her father, was devastated. She says that her father always made her feel protected and loved; no matter what Lois did, he was her number one supporter and cheerleader. After he died, Lois felt as though she had lost her 'safety zone' and quickly fell into a serious reactive depression; all she wanted to do was withdraw from the world and remain in the safety of her own apartment.

This mood couldn't have happened at a worse time because just then there was a shake-up in Lois' company. Her immediate boss was let go, and a young woman was brought in as a replacement. Lois had no history with this woman, who seemed to have zero tolerance for Lois' fragile emotional state. In fact, Lois' new boss seemed eager to replace all of the old employees with people who were younger and had no established loyalties to the earlier regime. Lois suddenly found herself under tremendous pressure to perform at what seemed to be an almost impossible level.

Lois, who was by now totally stressed, thought her mood, which alternated between depression and anger, was about as bad as it could get. But then Lois' boyfriend announced that he wanted to end the relationship. He said that he felt as though Lois had transferred her dependence on her father onto him, and he couldn't deal with it; he also said he couldn't handle her negative attitude and that she was no longer 'any fun.'

'What else can go wrong?' Lois asked several of her friends.

About a week later, she got her answer. Lois began to feel completely exhausted, so exhausted, in fact, that she could barely get out of bed. At first Lois blamed her fatigue on depression, but it quickly became apparent that this fatigue was different – deeper and more unyielding than anything she had ever before experienced. Something as simple as walking to the corner to buy a newspaper left her feeling depleted. When she went to a doctor, he diagnosed her malady as chronic fatigue syndrome. When she tried to take a leave of absence from work, they threatened to fire her. Lois' best friend was a lawyer so Lois was able to take legal action without it costing her a small fortune. So far, she has been able to get a two-month paid leave of absence for her illness. This has helped, but Lois knows it's just a matter of time before she will have to return to her office, and she's not sure if she will be able to do it.

Right now Lois is scared. In less than a year, she has suffered so many major losses – her father, her health, her boyfriend – one right after the other. If I were to talk to Lois and tell her that what she is going through is a valuable learning experience, she would probably have an impulse to slug me. And I would understand. Who wants to hear that the pain and suffering he or she is experiencing is part of a valuable lesson? I know I don't. Last week I stood in the rain on a busy highway with my disabled jeep waiting for AAA, late for an important appointment; I would have been infuriated if somebody had stuck his head out of the window of a passing car and yelled, 'It's a lesson, Surya!' And yet I have learned that all of life's trials and tribulations bring us tremendous opportunities for spiritual learning, growth, and meaningful connection.

I know men and women who have enough spiritual intelligence and discerning wisdom to look for and find the lessons in their travails. Chuck, a forty-five-year-old salesman, says that he never took the time to figure out what he might be doing wrong in his relationships with people until his business failed, his wife left him, and his teenage children stopped speaking to him. Chuck, who had always prided himself on his practical approach to life, forced himself to look at reality – at the interconnected patterns of cause and effect. If everyone he knew was angry at him, then he couldn't escape the logical conclusion that he was doing something to alienate those around him. He was thus able to learn, change, and grow from his difficulties. In this way, he reconciled with his loved ones.

My friend Deidra, now forty-one, has recovered from the anorexia that she lived with in her teens and early twenties. She told me that the worst thing about anorexia is that it made her feel separate and alienated from those around her. During the years when she struggled the most, Deidra spent much of her psychic energy concealing her illness and trying to make it seem as though she were eating normally. She says that being a full-blown anorexic was a truly terrifying experience. Nonetheless, she is grateful for what it taught her.

Deidra says that being anorexic made her aware not only of her own vulnerability, but of the vulnerability of everyone around her. Dealing with her own emotional problems gave her greater compassion and empathy for the emotional problems of others. She says this sense of everyone's suffering has permeated her awareness, her relationships, and her experience of life itself. She would not be who she is today if she hadn't known what it was like to struggle with an illness like anorexia.

Not that long ago I read a piece on the *New York Times* op-ed page. It was by James Stockdale, a retired Navy vice admiral. Stockdale had been a prisoner of war who spent four years in solitary confinement during the Vietnam War. To help put the experience of prisoners of war in perspective, James Stockdale quoted Aleksandr Solzhenitsyn:

> 'And it was only when I lay there on rotting prison straw that I sensed within myself the first stirrings of good. Gradually it was disclosed to me that the line separating good and evil passes not through states, nor between classes, nor between political parties either – but right through every human heart – and through all human hearts . . . And that is why I turn back to the years of my imprisonment and say, sometimes to the astonishment of those about me: "Bless you prison!"'

Admiral Stockdale's piece reminded me of the stories told to me by many of the Tibetan lamas who were jailed by the Chinese. One of them was my old friend, Lama Norlha, who now teaches in New York City as well as at Kalu Rinpoche's three-year retreat center in Wappinger Falls, New York. I first met Lama Norlha in Darjeeling in the early 1970s where we lived together in a small mountainside hermitage, and he would occasionally recount his experiences.

Back in 1959 after the Chinese invasion of Tibet, Lama Norlha was placed in a prison camp, which was really just a collection of tents on the frigid Tibetan steppes surrounded by barbed wire. Lama Norlha was there with several other Buddhist monks, tortured, hungry, cold, and unsure of whether they were going to survive. Yet he told me many times that these years as a prisoner were some of the best in his life.

Everything had been taken away from him except his spiritual brothers and his meditation practice. He realized that he had no past to return to and there was no future he could count on. All he could rely on was the present moment and the eternal truth of Dharma – as valid there as anywhere else. He realized that he could continue his spiritual practice sitting in the corner of his prison tent. I remember his saying, 'I had nothing else to do or be concerned about, for all had been stripped away.' This always seemed to me like a great lesson, reminding us that even in the most difficult circumstances if we summon our intentions and highest aspirations we can turn our minds to the Dharma.

Lama Norlha's time in prison ended happily when he had a dream in which his guru came to him and gave him instructions and specific directions on how to leave the prison camp without being detected. Following the dream's guidance, one night Lama Norlha and several other monks crept out under a corner of the tent, through the barbed wire enclosure, and headed for the sanctuary of India. In later life when he got quite busy as a teacher, chant leader, and temple builder, he would look back and give thanks for his years of intense meditation practice in a Chinese prison.

In his classic book *A Path with Heart,* my friend Jack Kornfield wrote:

> 'In difficulties, we can learn the true strength of our practice. At these times, the wisdom we have cultivated and the depth of our love and forgiveness is our chief resource. To meditate, to pray, to practice, at such times can be like pouring soothing balm onto the aches of our heart. The great forces of greed, hatred, fear, and ignorance that we encounter can be met by the equally great courage of our heart.
>
> 'Such strength of heart comes from knowing that the pain that we each must bear is a part of the greater pain shared by all that lives. It is not just "our" pain but *the* pain, and realizing this awakens our universal compassion.'

THE TRUTH OF 'PAIN' AND SUFFERING

The Buddha often reminded his followers that we are all going to experience illness, unexpected difficulties, aging, and death. We are all going to experience loss. This is a reality – a true 'fact of life.' We are all going to have many lessons in loss and suffering; no one is exempt. All religions and spiritual traditions delve into the nature and causes of human suffering. Sitting in a restaurant this summer I heard a lovely little girl, who couldn't have been more than five, ask the woman she was with, 'Margaret, why does God let bad things happen?' Margaret responded by saying that this was a question that had also plagued her for her entire life. Why do bad things happen? Isn't that a question that plagues all of our lives?

The little girl in the restaurant appeared to be a child of privilege, wonderfully dressed, and surrounded by a group of adults who clearly adored her and thought she was pretty special. Even so, at her young age, she was asking that age-old question. Afterward, I spoke briefly with one of the adults at the table and asked if they had any idea what specifically was disturbing the little girl. I was told that the child lived in Colorado and was very aware of the killings at Columbine High School. A question that the child often asked was why God allowed guns, bombs, and other instruments of violence.

All religious and spiritual traditions have tried to give us reasons as to why we live in an imperfect world. Many of these are buried in myths and legends that provide symbolic explanations. Here in the West, our Judeo-Christian tradition points to Adam and Eve in the Garden of Eden. When Adam and Eve followed the advice of the serpent, they lost their spot in the Garden. By giving into the snake, which represents temptation and desire, Adam and Eve taste the forbidden fruit of knowledge, which implies the knowledge of good and evil – dualism and an awareness of being separate from the Divine. They thus become *self*-conscious. The spiritual path that they (and each of us) must thus follow is one that brings them through the initial childlike state of nonindividuation and along the path that eventually brings them to independence, autonomous choice, and ultimately to reunion with the Divine principle, the true source and ground of our being.

This corresponds to our own nontheistic Buddhist cosmology in which it is generally taught that we begin in ignorance and dualism and end in enlightenment and oneness. Because of our delusions, we suffer. When we recognize enlightenment, we realize everlasting peace.

All life contains both joy and sorrow. We would like to concentrate on the joy and forget the sorrow, but how much more spiritually skillful it is to use everything we meet in life as grist for the mill of awakening. Chogyam Trungpa Rinpoche used to say that the more shit you encounter along the path, the better your spiritual flowers will grow – so long as you know how to use the shit as fertilizer. We used to joke about this, calling it the 'Manure Principle.' In Tibetan Buddhism, we call this having 'vajra' (diamond) teeth. With vajra teeth, we can grind everything we encounter into dust and digest it as easily as pablum; thus all our experiences become the equivalent of food to nourish and nurture the spirit.

When we apply this approach to life's ups and downs, we develop tremendous fearlessness, curiosity, and a greater passion for living. This vajra approach reflects the tantric principle of transforming even the greatest poisons into wisdom. The example often given is that of the wild peacocks found in India's deserts. The peacocks thrive on poisonous snakes; in fact the more poisonous snakes they eat, the bigger, more colorful their tail plumes become. This approach is very unlike that of the individual in the spiritual ivory tower who observes the world from afar. Instead, the tantric spiritual warrior jumps into the fray by leaping into the ocean of bullshit and swimming, sometimes even becoming a lifesaver.

There is an ancient Tibetan Buddhist practice that trains us in taking all of the 'shit' – the suffering, heartache, and pain – the world has to offer and using it as fertilizer for greater spiritual transformation. It is called 'Turning Happiness and Suffering into the Path of Enlightenment.'

TURNING HAPPINESS AND SUFFERING INTO THE PATH OF ENLIGHTENMENT

Going through my old notes from my late, great teacher His Holiness Dudjom Rinpoche on the Nyingmapa practice of accepting suffering as part of the path of enlightenment, I found scribbled in my Tibetan text's margins the following quote from Dudjom Rinpoche's son, Thinley Norbu Rinpoche:

'Same taste is the main precept. Seek to recognize that inherent wisdom or awareness is present and unaltered in both happiness and suffering. Understand that happiness no longer benefits, and suffering no longer hurts, through the experience of the same taste of all phenomenal appearances.'

Most of us spend our lives seeking pleasure and trying to avoid pain. What Lama Thinley Norbu was telling us to understand is that innate nondual awareness is present in all of us, in all circumstances. We must learn to practice it in all circumstances, whether they be favorable or unfavorable.

The Buddha's life is often used as an example of this principle: He experienced great extremes of austerity and discomfort as well as respect and adoration, yet his intention to help others remained constant, and his mind was steady no matter what the outward circumstances.

> *'In the absolute expanse of awareness*
> *All things are blended into that single taste –*
> *But, relatively, each and every phenomenon*
> *is distinctly, clearly seen.*
> *Wondrous!'*
>
> – Lama Shabkar,
> translated by Matthieu Ricard

In this life, we cannot expect to avoid pain, suffering, illness, or loss. We can, however, train our minds so that we are better able to let go rather than hang onto life's problems; we can lead our lives so that the difficulties we face become stepping stones rather than stumbling blocks on the path to enlightenment.

We can use lemons to make lemonade.

The Practice of Accepting Suffering as the Path to Enlightenment Offers the Following Teachings:

I. LET GO OF THE IDEA OF TELLING YOURSELF THAT YOU DON'T WANT SUFFERING; INSTEAD FOCUS ON THE FOLLOWING THOUGHT: WHATEVER DIFFICULTIES LIFE BRINGS, I WILL NOT BE ANXIOUS ABOUT THEM.

Anxiety and fear is often the worst part of any negative experience. My teachers would always say that it's a waste of time to be anxious about suffering. If you are able to heal the conditions that create difficulties, then your problems are resolved. If you are unable to change anything, it's not going to do you any good to be distressed. Anxiety about life's problems and your personal unhappiness can create even greater unhappiness, as well as stress-related illnesses. Concentrate your efforts on calming and freeing the mind. Contentment and fulfillment is right there, within yourself.

2. EMBRACE YOUR DIFFICULTIES AND APPRECIATE THEM FOR PROVIDING NEW WAYS TO GROW SPIRITUALLY. TRY TO THINK OF THE POSITIVE BENEFITS AND SPIRITUAL LESSONS THAT TROUBLES CAN ALMOST CERTAINLY PROVIDE. HERE ARE SOME OF THEM:

✳ Very few people begin a spiritual journey because they are blissfully happy. In fact, men and women are typically drawn to the spiritual path because they want help in dealing with difficulties. Each challenge in our lives opens the possibility of awakening our Buddhist heart.

✳ When we are going through dark times, we are better able to let go of egotism and arrogance. Difficulties can help us grow in patience, understanding, and humility; they can help us seek out meaningful connection.

✳ This is an ideal time for self-reflection and an examination of those ways in which we have contributed to our own problems – our own karma. Are any of our current difficulties, for example, caused by our own carelessness and lack of mindfulness?

✳ When our troubles seem overwhelming, often we can use this as a way of growing our compassion for others. Reflect on the millions of others who – just like you – are going through tough times right now. Empathize with these brothers and sisters with whom you share so many emotions.

THINK OF YOUR DIFFICULT TIMES AS SPIRITUAL TRAININGS

My enlightened Dzogchen master, His Holiness Dilgo Khyentse Rinpoche, said:

> *'Difficulties are like the ornament*
> *of a good practitioner.*
> *Dharma is not practiced perfectly*
> *amidst pleasant circumstances.'*

It's a fact: When we use our difficulties as a way to train our minds and transform our attitudes, we can overcome anxiety and fear; we thus cultivate virtues like forbearance, humility, and acceptance. In this way we become stronger, more balanced, and mentally stable. The Tibetan Buddhist teachers are so firmly convinced that this kind of challenging training can help one overcome emotions like fear and anxiety that they do meditation training at night in cemeteries and charnal grounds. They encourage practitioners to step up and face inner fears and use them as a propellant to contemplative energy.

When I first encountered this practice in Asia, I didn't really understand it, but eventually I came to see the spiritual benefits. When I lived in Darjeeling with my lamas, one very snowy winter it became too cold in the mountains, and I went south to visit Benares (Varanasi) on the Indian plains. There I lived along the banks of the Ganges River. Each evening a yogi friend and I would go to the stone steps of the ghat along the riverbank at one end of the city. There Hindus from around the globe would come to die and be cremated in their sacred river, as well as to watch the burning funeral pyres that illumed each night. The meditations I did at this awesome site were among the best I have ever experienced.

It was more than twenty-five years ago, but I remember as if it were yesterday the aura of severe solemnity and sacred awe surrounding these sunset proceedings. Not that I ever had a camera with me in India in those days, but I remember noticing that there were no tourists snapping photos or filming. The taking of pictures was absolutely prohibited in order to protect the sanctity of the funeral rite and the privacy of the grieving families who were present. The cremations generally occurred at dusk. Huge ravens and crows waited atop the old stone parapets of the ancient city walls and river-bank battlements, hoping for stray morsels of human flesh to pick up and carry away. Vultures loomed in the distance on the desert sands just across the wide, muddy, slow-flowing Ganges.

At first I was fearful. I remember the sickly sweet, gluey odor of burning flesh. It was frightening. And the first time I saw the corpse's distended limbs sticking out from the white gauze as the fire burnt away the shroud and the sinews dried up, pulling the hands and feet into various directions until they were extending out from the funeral pyre, I was shocked and speechless. I felt – and I still feel it viscerally – that my own body was mere firewood on the pyre of this world, this life. But the most frightening moment of all came when the eldest son of the deceased stepped forward with a large, stout stick in his hand. Alongside him was an old Brahmin priest who was intoning mantras and sprinkling consecrated water on the pyre. Bowing down to his late father's flaming corpse, the son chanted a prayer, and then raised the stick and brought it down on the corpse's skull with a sharp crack – to liberate the soul upward into Lord Shiva's embrace, as the Brahmins explained to me later.

My immediate reaction was to worry; I felt like I would become polluted or ill by contact with this scene. I was also afraid of the leprous beggars with raw exposed wounds, who lined the streets. Yet as a spiritual seeker on the path in India, I could not help but return night after night to sit on one of the cold stone temple parapets surrounding the proceedings. There I would meditate and observe the goings on, like a spectator in some Dante-esque netherworld.

This was good for me. I was twenty-two, and here, for the first time in my young and fairly privileged life, I had come face to face with the nitty-gritty facts of life and death. I realized my kinship with all who live – with all who live and die. At first it was frightening and fearsome, as well as awe inspiring. I was simply afraid – of what I could not exactly say: of the specter of death, I suppose; of being tainted or infected with death; of facing the fact of my own mortality; of ghosts, perhaps. It was mostly an unformed, unspoken fear. But soon, it became just part of my daily evening meditation – a sacred Benares sunset rite in which I could participate. It became a part of my practice, not that different from my habit of going to morning and evening chant services at Saint Ananda Mayee's ashram-temple overlooking the river at another, more gentle part of the riverside city. My original fear turned gradually into reverence and appreciation for the mystery of life, and for the natural unfolding of the process of life and death. I found that I was able to become more contemplative and less reactive and emotional about the spectacle, which to Western eyes initially seemed macabre.

By the time I was ready to return to my teacher's monastery in Darjeeling that spring, my attitude had changed. Often I would find myself sitting with the last straggling mourners, Brahmin priests, lepers, and eager crows long after the last glow of sunset had faded and the embers of the cremation pyres had begun to subside; by then night would be well advanced with the moon high over the Ganges. I think this experience helped me understand more clearly why Buddha said, 'Death is my guru; death is my greatest teacher. Death, impermanence, and mortality drove me to find that deathless peace beyond the snares of birth and death. To contemplate death and your own mortality is the ultimate meditation practice.'

The purpose of this kind of practice is to become so spiritually courageous and balanced that even the most difficult circumstances will reveal themselves as an opportunity for spiritual growth and deeper life-learning – what I like to call 'true higher education.' We Buddhists don't consider this morbid or negative in any way. This is not about seeking death; it's about embracing the opportunities that our precious lives provide even during the darkest, most frightening hours. It deepens and broadens our spiritual intelligence. In this way we become closer to absolute fearlessness and spiritual power.

BECOMING MORE BALANCED
AND CALM

All Buddhist teachers, and I am no exception, point out that all of our happiness as well as all of our despair arise from the mind. When we search for happiness and an end to suffering, the only place to look is within the mind itself. We each contain within ourselves all that we need for personal joy, bliss, wisdom, equanimity, and peace. There is no reason to look to externals or anywhere else. When one truly embraces this thought, there is nothing to fear. We are truly free.

Until we reach this level of spiritual peace, we are in some ways always at the mercy of external circumstances. We will continue to be affected by all events, great and small. The Tibetan text on turning unhappiness into the spiritual path says that 'our hair is tangled in a tree,' meaning that we are bound up in external circumstances that take over and leave us tied up. In a long prayerful poem, Dudjom Rinpoche wrote, 'May I tie around my own head the lead rope that is attached to my own nose,' meaning may we realize autonomy and self-mastery, and not always be at the mercy of things outside ourselves.

My teachers would often remind us that obstacles and problems could be viewed as blessings that should not be avoided. Difficulties help free us from our attachment to how we want things to be. In short, they help free us from the fantasies that keep us from awakening to the joy of enlightenment, the bliss of what is. When we take this approach, we find that we are able to see and appreciate the lessons and opportunities in each experience. This applies to both the positive and the negative. Just as we are often fearful and anxious of negative experiences, and thus fail to reap the lessons that are there for us, so too we can so easily overlook and deny the blessings and simple, everyday joys in our lives.

Many seekers today, for example, complain about the level of stress they are under from the pressures of schedules and responsibilities. Often this stress is generated by the demands we place on ourselves to be better parents, friends, partners, employees, employers, neighbors – in short, to be better people. Perhaps instead of viewing our obligations as burdens, we could incorporate them into a spiritual practice with a little prayer that further emphasizes our commitment to the awakened awareness and goodness of heart embodied in the precious Bodhicitta.

We cultivate and reinforce our compassionate intentions to do good and to help, not harm, others. Because we love and care about ourselves, we naturally learn more and more to extend ourselves to others since they are really not much different than we are. In this way, each of us can transform and re-condition much of our own selfish, egotistical behavior, and be more of a peacemaker and bearer of love, shedding light wherever we go.

We all long for spiritual blessings, protection, and wholeness. Yet it is not often appreciated how many blessings we all have within us and in our lives. We remember the old spiritual admonishment 'Count your blessings' as we try not to overlook all that we have been given. Moreover we could practice giving blessings to ourselves and our own hopes and ideals; we could freely offer blessings to others from the fullness of our hearts. We need to overcome any tendencies to be stingy with our blessings, mistakenly assuming that blessings come from someone else. Each of us is a blessed one – you too!

When we look at everything we are experiencing – good and bad – with sacred outlook and nonjudgmental awareness, we further enhance our personal spiritual growth.

THE PRACTICE OF PURE PERCEPTION

One of the unique practices in Tibetan Buddhism is called 'dak-nang,' the practice of pure perception or sacred outlook. In this practice, we focus our energy on seeing this world as a perfect Buddha Field – a paradise-like realm – with all beings as Buddhas. This is a wonderful practice to keep in mind whenever we find ourselves strongly liking or not liking an experience, an event, a feeling, or a person.

We can further put this into perspective in the bigger context of what Tibetan Buddhists refer to as the Great Perfection teachings or Dzogchen. This is the ultimate revelation through which we recognize that everything that arises both within and outside us is the stately process of what we call the 'Dharmakaya,' or absolute dimension – the radiance of absolute truth or naked reality, stripped of illusions and conceptual imputations.

What we mean by Dharmakaya is that Buddha-nature, or primordial luminosity, is manifested and expressed through every element of our world and existence.

In short, everything is Dharmakaya – everything, including our emotions, whether they are healthy or unhealthy, positive or negative, constructive or destructive. The things we like or don't like, including physical sensations such as pain or pleasure, are all part of the blessed, radiant Dharmakaya or Buddha-nature at work – or better yet, Buddha-nature at play.

What this means is that all beings are the Buddhas in this Buddha Field. The earth is the altar, and we are the deities sitting, standing, and walking on the altar. Everything is sacred; all are holy; everything is perfectly radiant and stainless in the Buddhavision-like light of the natural Great Perfection. This is the perspective of 'dak-nang,' the practice of pure perception.

My late friend John Blofeld was a Buddhist author, scholar, and translator; he lived for many years in China and Tibet during the 1950s and '60s. Eventually, during the 1970s, he settled into married life in Bangkok with his Thai wife. Once when I visited him there, John told me how difficult it was for him to get acclimated to living in such a bustling, noisy city after living for decades in Himalayan monasteries and Chinese Taoist hermitages. He said that what he found particularly challenging was practicing his Tantric Green Tara Meditation for two hours in his Bangkok apartment each morning before leaving for his office.

In his apartment, John had created and decorated a lovely Tara shrine and meditation room. The room was filled with exquisite sacred art that he had accumulated over the years – beautiful statues of Buddha; small, delicate paintings; altar pieces; Chinese brocade; sacred texts; and rare books and manuscripts, along with antique offering bowls and lamps. But despite the beauty of his surroundings, John couldn't keep the discordant sounds of Bangkok morning traffic from coming through his window and interrupting his meditation.

John said the heavy traffic, especially the sounds of mufflerless truck engines and gear shifting combined with horns honking in the distance, really bugged him. After years of meditation practice and experience, he knew he could, and even should, be able to concentrate. Nonetheless, he found that he was unable either to block the intruding sounds from his mind or to integrate them into his awareness practice without being distracted or disturbed. The fact remained – he told me with a sheepish laugh – that the cacophony of the daily rush hour often made him long for his Himalayan retreats and the years of silence and solitude he had spent with his spiritual masters.

Then one day something 'clicked' into place. It must have been a blessing from the 'traffic gods' combined with that of his own lineage of guides and gurus, augmented of course by the good karma he'd accumulated by faithfully persevering despite the distracting noise. Whatever the reason, one morning while he was in his shrine room, meditating on Tara, he suddenly re-alized that all those honking horns, droning engines, and clunking gears didn't sound that much different from the blaring of Tibetan long horns and the clash of huge brass monastery cymbals wafting through his old hermitage window in Darjeeling, where John had studied Dzogchen with my own late master, Dudjom Rinpoche. In his master's monastery, John had found the sounds of the horns an enhancement to his morning meditation. Why should it be different now?

John told me that he suddenly realized – like awakening from a dream – that it was simply a matter of how he was perceiving those sounds – as distracting traffic noise, or as a celestial Tibetan ritual choir – that made all the difference. Until that moment, for no real reason other than his own interpretation superimposed upon things, he had found one set of sounds uplifting, and the other brought him down.

John then fully realized for the first time the secret of the Tibetan practice of pure perception – seeing all forms as rainbow energy, hearing all sounds as deities chanting mantras, and recognizing the Buddha light in everyone and everything. From that day on, John's morning prayers and Tara practice were totally transformed and absolutely blessed. The sacred sounds coming through his window may have been different from the sounds he had heard in his guru's distant Himalayan monastery, but – in his transformed vision – they were sacred nonetheless. Thus he found himself peacefully at home with his guru in Tara's Buddha Field, even amidst bustling Bangkok – a city that never sleeps.

THE PRACTICE OF PURE PERCEPTION / SACRED OUTLOOK – A MEDITATION

Let's put into practice our ideal of seeing, recognizing, and appreciating the light in everyone and everything, so that all that we experience becomes an integral part of our spiritual awareness – part and parcel of our awakened/enlightened heart.

Look around the room.
See it all in a fresh new light.
Experience what you are feeling in a new way.
Open up to the luminous energy by regarding the transparent, luminous insubstantiality of all forms and perceptions.
Breathe in light along with air,

and breathe out light again.

Visualize light pouring in like a river, along with your in breath, and gushing out along with your out breath.

Breathe the light in and out,
filling you up,
Emptying, cleansing, purifying . . .

Envision the place you are standing suffused with and surrounded by light, haloed as in a piece of sacred art.

Envision the people around you filled with light, surrounded by light, emanating bliss and de-light, like the sages or saints in a religious painting.

(This may seem fabricated, but I assure you it is simply a reflection of the actuality that is momentarily too subtle for most of us to perceive.)

Keep breathing the clear light in and out, like a continuous circle or wheel of luminosity that turns inside and out, day and night.

Recognize others as being living Buddhas, gods or goddesses — all splendid and divine in their own right, in their own way, their own light.

Why be deterred by the mere appearance of their particular form or manifestation?

Why be deterred by the illusory interaction their forms and personalities have with our own?

Deep down we are all Buddhas by nature,
perfectly pure and complete luminous beings
of pure light and energy.

Honor their enlightened Buddha-nature, their innate divinity.
See them in a new light,

beyond personal distinctions, preferences and discriminations.
Breathing light, out and in, within and without,
filling and emptying our noble heart
which is pure light, illumining oneself, illumining others,
illumining the whole world:
Rest in that glorious inner sphere
of spiritual splendor,
seeing everything in an utterly new light.

Now take this sacred vision out to others who are not present.
Envision your parents, mates, colleagues, children, and neighbors
in this new light.
Embrace them with light.
Let's take this outside into the world.
Keep breathing the light in and out, back and forth,
circulating the cosmic energy throughout your own system.
As you leave the premises, gaze benevolently upon
whoever first crosses your path — human, animal, or winged
insect.
Breathe in the light, then breathe it out to them,
embracing them in the radiant light of pure perception, of clear
seeing.
Notice whatever may come up and intrude
upon seeing these Buddha-like spiritual beings.
See through that momentary obscuration veiling their inner
splendor
to appreciate their deeper truth and blessed being.

Carry this new way of seeing home with you, and bring it into your family, your workplace, your daily commute.

Keep breathing light. Breathe it in and renew yourself. Breathe it out and embrace others.

Hold your employees or boss in this light, and see how it feels. See how it changes your relationships with others, even though they don't know you are doing this.

How different this is from how we usually see things and people!

This is how we cultivate pure perceptions and achieve a sacred outlook that embraces everything and everyone – from the sublime to the mundane, from the glad to the sad – in the vast mandala of the awakened heart-mind. Amazing! Wonder-full!

CHAPTER TEN

Learning to Love What We Don't Like

A Disciple asked Rabbi Shmelke: 'We are commanded to love our neighbor as ourself. How can I do this, if my neighbor has wronged me?'

The Rabbi answered: 'You must understand these words right. Love your neighbor like something which you yourself are. For all souls are one. Each is a spark from the original soul, and this soul is wholly inherent in all souls, just as your soul is in all the members of your body. If your hand makes a mistake and strikes you, would you then hit your hand with a stick and thus increase your pain? It is the same with your neighbor. If you punish him, you only hurt yourself.'

The Disciple went on asking: 'But if I see a man who is wicked before God, how can I love him?'

'Don't you know,' said Rabbi Shmelke, 'that the original soul came out of the essence of God, and that every human soul is a part of God? And will you have no mercy on him when you see that one of his holy sparks has been lost in a maze, and is almost stifled?'

— Martin Buber, *Tales of the Hassidim*

Why should we learn to love and connect with people and other beings we don't particularly like? Why should we love those who hurt us and cause us pain? Why should anyone want to love people like Hitler, Pol Pot, Stalin, or Idi Amin? How can we learn to love terrorists and people who cause war or genocide? How can we love drivers who are angry, careless, or drunk? How can we love men and women who are intolerant, petty, and unkind to fellow beings? How can we learn to love people who grate on our nerves? How can we learn to love mosquitoes, snakes, and slimy creatures we don't want anywhere near us? Why? Why? Why? How? How? How? When it comes to love, there are a lot of whys and hows.

There is at least one basic, simple, universal, and ultimately self-serving reason to love: The act of loving is naturally healing in and of itself. Negative feelings like anger and hate make us contract and close up; they can even make us feel and be sick. On the other hand, the more we love, the better we feel. In short, loving others is a way of loving – and healing – ourselves. When we send out pure loving-kindness, it reverberates back; sending love and receiving love go hand in hand. We love in order to feel love. That's why we love.

Being open and loving is a great feeling, isn't it? It's certainly a better feeling than hatred! What do we think about when we first hear the word 'love'? Do we think of our child, our mate, our pets? Do we think of parents, siblings, or friends? Do we think of nature, a tree in the backyard perhaps, or a favorite vacation spot that brings us joy? When we talk about Dharma, spirituality, or truth and love, it really all comes down to the same thing – an exquisite appreciation of something, someone, or a certain moment in life, an appreciation of something that is beautiful and meaningful to us. That's really what we love, isn't it? How we feel in that moment. We might say we love a person or a place, but if we really look into it, what we are probably loving is how we feel when this person is with us.

Buddhism teaches that love is the antidote to anger, aversion, hatred, and fear. Buddhism also has something to say about *how* to love; it teaches us that mindfulness – authentic being – is the path to love. This answers the question of how to love. Being mindful in the present moment brings us to an understanding of 'what is.' Mindfulness allows us to touch our own innate Buddha-nature; it allows us to see and touch the Buddha-nature in everyone we meet. In his extraordinary book *Living Buddha, Living Christ,* Thich Nhat Hanh writes:

'When we are mindful, touching deeply the present moment, we can see and listen deeply, and the fruits are always understanding, acceptance, love, and the desire to relieve suffering and bring joy . . . To me, mindfulness is very much like the Holy Spirit. Both are agents of healing. When you have mindfulness, you have love and understanding, you see more deeply, and you can heal the wounds in your own mind. The Buddha was called the

King of Healers. In the Bible, when someone touches Christ, he or she is healed. It is not just touching a cloth that brings about a miracle. When you touch deep understanding and love, you are healed.'

'LOVE' IS DIFFERENT FROM 'LIKE'

When I was a young man, I thought love was always supposed to come easily and naturally. Then I discovered that in life, we are sometimes called upon to love people and situations that we don't really like. That's when love becomes more demanding and challenging.

During the 1980s I spent eight years in extended retreat, in a secluded Tibetan monastery in France. People often ask me what was the most important thing I got out of those years in a Dzogchen retreat center, so I've thought about this question a lot. There were twenty-three of us cloistered together in a forest retreat. Some of us didn't know each other that well to start out with so it was a little like entering into an arranged marriage. There were many issues on which we didn't always agree. But I eventually learned that I could love and care about people whose opinions and habits I didn't always like or agree with. For me this was an important lesson that reinforced, in a very personal way, the Buddha's teachings on the nature of love and compassion. It was extraordinarily peace-making in my own mind and has stood me in good stead years later as I am more actively engaged in modern life and religious politics with all its trials and vicissitudes.

Spiritual teachings of all the great traditions reiterate time and time again that loving opens our hearts to acceptance and forgiveness. For me, this bespeaks an inner equanimity that is capable of appreciating all things, even as they fluctuate and morph into one kind of experience after another. Love is where we live and come from, not just what we are heading toward. It's like how we were when we were children – filled with wonder and appreciation, and open to everything. We come to perceive things with fresh eyes and ears. Everything is new and therefore miraculous and marvelous. We love it. We can embrace life fully all along the entire length of her body.

Walking the spiritual path means that we are trying to learn to love universally – not just our mates, friends, or children, but everyone. We are trying to learn to love things just as they are, for this is 'truth' according to Buddha's definition. We are trying to learn to love through whatever experience we have – good, bad, or indifferent. This is a wisdom love, not just based on momentary passion, feeling, and self-reference, but rooted far more deeply in genuine caring, empathy, and unselfishness.

LEARNING DEEPER ACCEPTANCE AND FORGIVENESS

When we talk about love, we are talking about something that is quite soulful, not abstract – not just 'ah, emptiness!' or a philosophical 'The Infinite.' When some of us try to

incorporate more loving-kindness and compassionate practices into our lives, I think we are often doing it because we
want to fix something that's going wrong in our own lives.
Instead, I think we should focus on appreciating everything
and opening up to life's experiences with greater tolerance,
forbearance, and acceptance. In order to get to that place, of
course, we have to begin to work on forgiving everyone their
shortcomings, even ourselves.

When I was in elementary school, I was a real hellion and
often in trouble. I always seemed to get a red F in conduct,
and although my other grades were much better, I was so
overactive that finally they demoted me. I was sent out of the
advanced class to another class to be with a group of kids who,
like me, were all incipient truants and hell raisers. Still I was
among the worst. The teacher of that spirited class seemed to
have a real talent for dealing with troublemakers. At every
opportunity, he would take us outside so we could let off
energy; it was sort of like we were majoring in playground. I
started to like it!

What I remember most about this teacher, Mr LaRocca,
was that he was a tough, strong guy, who wasn't intimidated
by a couple of dozen rowdy kids. Once I created such a distur-
bance in class that he put me outside in the hallway; of course
I simply ran away and played outside on the ball field. Then
he put me under his desk. That's where I lived for a while.
Crunched under the desk and in the dark, I couldn't do
anything; I was stuffed down between his shins and a wooden
hard place. I don't remember how long I stayed there, but
certainly until I gave in at least a little bit. Finally he put my

desk right next to his, facing the blackboard where he kept a big eye on me. This was definitely the truant's seat.

At first I saw Mr LaRocca as being a real pain. He was my enemy, and I was out to get him with as much zeal as any hyperactive kid could muster; I also thought he was out to get me. But gradually my attitude began to change. He found out that I was interested in sports, so he took me to the library and showed me how to find and borrow the sports magazines and biographies; he encouraged me to find a way to combine the learning process with things I was naturally interested in. Most important, he didn't give up on me. Eventually I came to appreciate and even love him. Today, of course, I realize that he was a blessing in disguise. My enemy was really my best friend. That man may have saved my life. James LaRocca is the only elementary school teacher I ever visited again, years later. I still remember him with love.

Of course my grade school teacher wasn't a very threatening enemy. As we mature and become adults, we often find ourselves facing enemies who have the potential to be far more lethal and damaging. We come face to face with people whose motivations seem to be destructive, deceitful, and hurtful; we are forced to confront enemies in the form of illnesses and tragedies, such as serious accidents, cancer, heart disease, and AIDS. Some of us have chronic pain from arthritis; others have chronic fatigue. Our enemies may appear in the form of bad relationships, or addictive or self-destructive lifestyles. These are also our enemies, and this is tough stuff.

Shantideva, known as the Gentle Angel Master, said that our enemies are our greatest teachers. Our enemies teach us patience, equanimity, and love. In this way, our enemies also teach us forgiveness and acceptance.

Forgiveness and acceptance also play major roles in many Buddhist teaching tales. I've always liked a Zen story about forgiveness and acceptance in Paul Reps' classic book *Zen Flesh, Zen Bones*. It's about a Zen master named Shichiri, who, one evening while he is reciting sutras, is interrupted by a thief with a sharp sword. Shichiri, who is very involved with what he is doing, tells the thief, 'Do not disturb me. You can find the money in that drawer.' Shichiri goes back to the sutras for a minute, but then he calls out again, 'Don't take it all. I need some to pay taxes with tomorrow.'

The thief takes most of the money, and as he leaves, Shichiri says, 'Thank a person when you receive a gift.' The surprised intruder thanks him and leaves.

Within a week, the man is caught and confesses what he has done. When he is brought to trial, Shichiri, who has been called as a witness, says: 'This man is no thief, at least as far as I am concerned. I gave him the money, and he thanked me for it.'

The Zen master Shichiri's ability to accept and forgive so impressed the thief that it caused him to undergo an inner transformation. Once he was released from prison, he went straight to Shichiri and became his disciple.

It is possible to recognize that we can detest someone's actions without detesting the person; we can hate the sin without hating the sinner, as is often said. I once saw a mother chastising her small child saying, 'You're a *good* child, but you just did a *bad* thing.' I think this is a distinction most of us need to recognize. It's possible to judge and condemn the action, not the person doing it. We can disagree with what someone says while we continue to respect this person's right to say it. In this way, we can drop some of the burdens of anger, bitterness, and resentment that we carry around with us. We can love more broadly and still maintain our integrity and common sense.

Forgiveness is a major part of love and acceptance. When we carry around the heavy weights of anger and unforgiveness, we hurt ourselves. Rabbi Harold Kushner said that if after two days you still haven't forgiven someone for something, it becomes your responsibility. And he was talking about the most grievous things, not just about somebody cutting you off on a traffic circle. I think Rabbi Kushner's suggestion of two days is a good one to follow, difficult as that may seem. As Buddhists we recognize that whatever someone else does is their karma to be dealt with. But if we hang on to the anger past that two-day limit, it becomes our karma too, and we are victimizing ourselves.

Whom Do You Need to Forgive?

Do you have a personal list of people whom you need to forgive? Don't we all? My friend Greta made a list of some of the people she had trouble forgiving. Here it is:

✳ Mother – for filling her daughter's head full of fantasies about the possibility of Prince Charming; for fault finding and nagging; for generally childish behavior.

✳ Father – for being 'distant'; for abandoning his family emotionally, and for not protecting Greta from her mother.

✳ Brother – for being unkind and picking on her when she was still very little.

✳ First husband – for having an affair that ended their marriage.

✳ Former sister-in-law – for knowing what her brother (Greta's ex-husband) was doing and looking the other way, making Greta feel even more betrayed.

✳ Employer – for his bad temper and for taking advantage of her willingness to work hard.

✳ Friends – for being self-centered and failing to give adequate support.

✳ Self – for gaining weight and not being able to lose it.

If you were to examine your heart and your psyche, would you find a list of people and things you have difficulty forgiving? What would it look like? What grudges or vendettas are you harboring? What old prejudices are you carrying? Do you have memories of past events that fill you with hurt or rage every time you think about them? There is no need to feel guilty that these exist; simply examine these old memories and bring them into awareness. In the clear light of incandescent awareness, the old-fashioned bogeyman goes away and disappears; on the other hand, what stays unconscious continues to afflict us.

Often our deepest pockets of unforgiveness and loathing are directed at ourselves. We remember something we did or something we said, and we flinch at our behavior. We ask ourselves how we could have been so stupid, hurtful, or just plain unconscious.

In order to start the process of forgiveness, we let our minds soften up and we try to become more resilient and less rigid. We try to let go of our attachment to ideas about the past; we try to look at the world with more open and forgiving minds. When Greta, for example, allows herself to look at her mother with greater forgiveness, she sees that her mother was simply doing the best she could; from this point of view Greta is able to remember all the kind things her mother did, including the times that her mother drove her and her friends to their various after school activities. She is able to develop a more realistic and balanced view of her relationship with her mother. In this way she begins to let go of her attachment to her resentments, and focus instead on observing her life and what is happening moment to moment. As she begins to get psychologically up to date with herself, a lot of old baggage and burdens fall away, and she feels greater freedom.

Some of us have a personal history filled with people and events that loom so large in our heads that it seems as though forgiveness is barely possible. When I was teaching in Israel a few years ago, people often told me that they could never forgive Hitler and the Nazis. After I spoke about karmic responsibility and the law of cause and effect, some started shouting from the audience, 'The Bible says, "an eye for an eye, a tooth for a tooth."' One angry audience member would egg on another, and then become even more furious. What can you say in the face of that kind of energy? It's difficult to discuss the universal law of reaping what we sow in the face of such virulent, unprocessed passions. When someone has harmed or killed a loved one, forgiveness can seem like a mighty challenge, and yet I think it's a challenge that needs to be met if we are to find any level of peace or happiness. We are up to the challenge.

What we try to do is make a spiritually intelligent distinction between forgiveness and forgetfulness. We should forgive even as we remember and learn from history. The past informs and conditions the present in ways great and small. If you, for example, know you are allergic to peanuts, mindfulness reminds you to avoid the food that can make you ill. In the same way, although the Dalai Lama forgives the Chinese Communists in his heart, he is also very realistic about their intentions when it comes to Tibet and forgets nothing about their history together in his country.

On television we sometimes see interviews with parents who have lost their children at the hand of a drunk driver or some other tragedy, and who have gone on to try to make the world better for other children by forming or being active in organizations that help protect life. They haven't allowed themselves to become paralyzed and embittered with their anger and despair; instead they have transformed their terrible pain and grief into spiritual intentions which help them to live better with their loss. Even some close relatives of murdered loved ones have found it in their hearts to forgive convicted and condemned murderers and work for clemency for them. This is a truly spiritual statement on their part.

I love the story of the elderly Mississippi laundress named Osceola McCarty, who for years secretly saved the money she earned from scrubbing other people's clothes and then gave it to a scholarship fund to help young people go to college. She had a minimal education herself, and yet instead of being bitter at her own lost opportunities, she vowed to help others – and she did. In so doing, she helped transform the lives of others as well as her own.

The past is part of the present; the only way that we can heal the past is by transforming the present. Thich Nhat Hanh says, 'The ghosts of the past which follow us into the present also belong to the present moment. To observe them deeply, recognize their nature, and transform them, is to transform the past.'

Staying in the present moment is, of course, a central theme of the Buddhist path; remembering this helps us deal with haunting memories and those things that we have difficulty forgiving. Teaching his followers, the Buddha said:

> *'Do not pursue the past.*
> *Do not lose yourself in the future.*
> *The past no longer is.*
> *The future has not yet come.*
> *Looking deeply at life as it is*
> *in the very here and now,*
> *the practitioner dwells*
> *in stability and freedom.'*

THE ANCIENT PRACTICE OF GIVING
AND RECEIVING

Approximately a thousand years ago, an Indian Buddhist abbot named Atisha was invited to Tibet to help teach the Dharma. Legend has it that at that time Atisha had a dream in which the exalted female Buddha Tara appeared to him, telling him that if he went to Tibet, the Dharma would be greatly enhanced but his own life would be shortened by a dozen years. Atisha decided that the longevity of the Dharma was more important to the world than his own mortal existence. Although he was already sixty years of age, Atisha then travelled by foot through the treacherous mountain passes of Northern India and Nepal until he arrived in Tibet, where he spent the remaining years of his life orally transmitting teachings and founding the Kadampa school of Tibetan Buddhism. Atisha's teachings form the basis of Tibet's renowned Mahayana Mind Training, also known in Tibet as Lo-jong. These Attitude Transformation Trainings revolve around the indispensable concept of Bodhicitta and the Bodhisattva ideal.

Some hundred years after Atisha's death, a monk named Geshe Chékawa was in his lama's room one day. There, on a table near the head of his teacher's bed, he noticed a single sentence that was written on parchment. It said, 'Give all the profit and gain to others, and unselfishly accept all the blame and loss.' Geshe Chékawa's hair stood on end; he was so inspired by the unselfish message of these lines that he set out to try to find who had authored them. In his travels, Geshe Chékawa finally met a leper who told him that the enlightened Master Atisha was dead, but that he knew of someone who was a direct lineage disciple. In this way, Geshe Chékawa came to meet the learned layman named Drom, lineage holder of the Kadampa school.

When Geshe Chékawa questioned Lama Drom about the importance of the teaching contained in the sentence he had found in his teacher's room, Lama Drom replied that the practice of this teaching was absolutely essential to enlighten-ment. 'Give all the profit and gain to others, and unselfishly accept all the blame and loss' formed the heart-essence of his own spiritual practice.

Geshe Chékawa apprenticed himself to Lama Drom for a dozen years, learning all he could. As time went on Geshe Chékawa began to share these teachings, first with a com-munity of lepers because he felt a debt of gratitude to the leper who had helped him find Atisha's disciple. Tibetan oral tradition tells us that as these lepers practiced with Geshe Chékawa, they began to be healed.

In the meantime, Geshe Chékawa had a very skeptical and cynical brother who had never shown any interest in learning about the Dharma. Nonetheless, Chékawa's brother couldn't help noticing the transformation occurring with the lepers. The brother thus began to hide outside an open window to hear Chékawa's teachings. Eventually he too began to prac-tice what was being taught. When Geshe Chékawa noticed the change in his brother's attitude, he was truly impressed. If the teachings could work even for his hard-hearted brother, they could work for anyone, he thought. And his faith and conviction in the Lo-jong practice was further strengthened.

Thus inspired, Geshe Chékawa began to write down Atisha's teachings, based on what Lama Drom remembered. These teachings are known in Tibet as Atisha's Seven Points of Mind Training. Out of these teachings has emerged the unique Tibetan practice called 'tonglen' or giving and receiving.

Tonglen evolves from the sentence 'Give all profit and gain to others and unselfishly accept all blame and loss.' This concept of giving away 'the good, the desirable' and accepting 'the bad, the undesirable' is quite foreign to Western ears. Most of us genuinely want the opposite; we want to breathe in only light and breathe out darkness.

In fact, this idea of breathing in 'the good' and breathing out 'the bad' is at the center of many New Age practices. Yet tonglen teaches us to do exactly the opposite. How can this be? This is the question many people ask when they first hear about tonglen.

Tonglen is one of the most misunderstood Tibetan Buddhist practices. In no way is it designed to make the practitioner ill or more afflicted. Its purpose is very simple: It is a mind training/attitude transformation practice meant to help us root out egotism, clinging, and dualism. It is a way to help us transform our attitudes toward those people and situations we naturally dislike, or even fear. In tonglen practice, we exchange ourselves with another; we use our mental powers to help us feel and identify with the afflictions of others. In this way, we learn to walk in someone else's shoes and better understand where others are coming from.

A belief, fundamental to the Christian faith, is that by his death, Jesus Christ took on the sins and burdens of the world. Tonglen is a Buddhist training that in many ways follows Jesus' noble ideal. Last year when I returned from a teaching trip, I received an e-mail from a woman that said in part:

'My dear lama,

I have a friend who is going through chemotherapy right now, which is causing her a lot of pain. Her suffering makes me feel help- less, and I want to find a way to comfort her. Could you please tell me how to pray and do the deeper tonglen practice so I can better take on some of her suffering? I would do anything to take on the pain if I could relieve her even half as much . . .'

The e-mail made me feel humble in the light of the writer's sincerity and natural goodness. It was apparent that she has a tender, compassionate, and loving heart. Most of us are doing tonglen because we want to be able to be as spontaneously caring as she is. Throughout the years, people have reported that tonglen practice has had a healing effect on themselves, on others, and on difficult situations and relationships. Nonetheless, although the letter writer is attracted to tonglen because she believes it might help her friend, tonglen's primary intent is to help heal the practitioner. It does this by helping us open our own inner loving hearts; it helps us be more accepting and forgiving toward both the desirable and undesirable aspects of life. In this way it gives us greater equa- nimity and peace, regardless of what is happening. For this reason, this is one of the best practices to deal with the most difficult situations in life, whether it's illness, a difficult mate, or an impossible job situation. It has helped me a great deal, especially when facing my greatest hardships.

In life, what we typically do is try to grasp what we want while we push away the undesirable. In Buddhist terminology this is known as attachment and aversion. By reversing these tendencies, tonglen helps us shake up our world and loosen the stranglehold of concepts such as 'like' and 'dislike,' or 'I want and I don't want.'

Beginning Tonglen Practice

'Whoever wishes quickly to become
A place of refuge for self and others,
Should undertake this sacred mystery;
To take the place of others, giving them his or her own.'
— From *The Way of the Bodhisattva*

Shantideva wrote *The Way of the Bodhisattva* over a thousand years ago. He said that the only way to make ourselves happy is to practice love and compassion, or Bodhicitta. Tonglen – the Practice of Giving and Receiving – is one of the principal Bodhicitta practices. It begins with an intention to open our hearts to others and also to ourselves, with the intention to learn to feel what others feel, to empathize and practice compassion. We want to allow the entire world into our hearts; we want to share what we have, what we are given. We willingly share ourselves.

We start by settling down as we would for any sitting meditation.

Get comfortable, get settled.

Loving-kindness meditations are aided by feelings of comfort and ease, so try to relax.

Use your breath to help you get settled in the present moment. Slowly, mindfully breathe in, and then breathe out through the nostrils. Breathe in gently and out gently.

Inhale . . .

Exhale . . . Relax.

TONGLEN PRACTICE – PART ONE

The traditional tonglen instructions tell us to open up to the practice by reflecting on the basic teachings of the Buddha:

✳ Be aware of the preciousness and opportunities provided by our human birth.

✳ Be aware of the fragile and impermanent nature of life – all life including our own.

✳ Be mindful of the implications of karma and our own intention to purify our actions.

TONGLEN PRACTICE – PART TWO

✳ MEDITATE ON THE OPEN NATURE OF REALITY

Things are not what they seem, nor are they otherwise. Everything changes; nothing remains the same. About this teaching, some simply say that we should 'regard everything as a dream.' We are trying to cultivate the mind of enlightenment – direct insight, or clear vision, into the transparent nature of self and all phenomena. This is the fundamental teaching of absolute Bodhicitta. About this, the modern-day teacher Pema Chodron writes, 'The way to reunite with Bodhicitta is to lighten up in your practice and in your whole life . . . That's the essential meaning of the absolute Bodhicitta slogans – to connect with the open, spacious quality of your mind, so that you can see that there's no need to shut down and make such a big deal about everything.'

At the beginning of any tonglen practice, rest in the empty, dreamlike, infinite nature of mind.

Then, the instructions tell us to:

❋ RIDE THE MOVING BREATH

Doing the meditation of 'sending and receiving,' we place our attention on the breath and inhale. Doing this, we visualize drawing in – taking upon ourselves – a black cloud of negativity. As we exhale, we visualize that we are giving out our goodness, our light – in short, the best part of ourselves. As we ride the moving breath, we visualize taking in the bad and exhaling the good – taking the burdens of others upon ourselves and giving away our good fortune and strength.

When they first hear about this practice, many people are confounded. They ask, 'Why would anyone want to breathe in the dark and breathe out the light?' But this practice, which goes against all our conditioning, provides an amazing tantric twist. It helps us face all those undesirable things we fear and try to avoid, instead of being deceived by mere appearances. Most of us have been conditioned to have a dualistic – this is good, this is bad – view of the world. After all, is darkness really bad, in any ultimate sense? Is light really good? By practicing tonglen, we begin to even out all our dualistic, judgmental views of the world. We begin to gain more inner detachment and balance. We naturally become more gentle and kind.

Many modern teachers advise that as we begin the tonglen practice – Riding the Breath, in and out – we start by focusing first on ourselves. It is easier to begin wishing well to ourselves before we begin the arduous task of evening out the differences we feel between ourselves and others. In this way, we begin approaching the spiritual ideal of treating others like ourselves by first allowing ourselves to be the recipients of our own compassionate intentions.

To do this, think about the various ways that you may feel that you need healing. Let's say, for example, that you feel confused, angry, or pained about an issue in your life.

Take this confusion, negativity, or pain and place it in front of you. Now, take a minute and allow yourself to become aware of the difficulty that your problem is causing you. Think about how healing it would be if you could be free of this negative energy. Continue breathing, and as you ride the breath, in and out, visualize that you are 'Hoovering' or vacuuming up all the negativity and anger you feel as if it were a cloud of black smoke. Now, on the out breath, send out your positive energy and blessings as a ray of light. Let your positive energy and blessings gently surround your problems, whatever they might be. Breathe in the dark, the smoke, anxiety, agitation, fog, pollution, and static. Breathe out the light, the clean air, the sound of silence, the joy, the blessings, and peace and love.

TONGLEN PRACTICE – PART THREE

✳ EXCHANGE SELF-AWARENESS FOR AWARENESS OF OTHERS

Tibet's first Dalai Lama, who lived from 1391–1475, said, 'Self-cherishing is said to be the source of all conflicts in this world. The cherishing of others is said to be the source of all happiness.' The traditional mind-training and tonglen instructions use the phrase 'Drive All Blames into One.' What this means is that egotistical self-cherishing is at the root of all our troubles. We are in constant conflict, incessantly trying to get what we want and avoid what we don't want. This attitude hasn't served us well. In fact, often we find that we simply get more and more caught up in vicious and unsatisfying cycles.

As we try to reverse this tendency, we breathe in and breathe out. We keep breathing and relaxing, gentling our energies, our bodies, our minds, and our spirits. We begin first with a person we care about. We place this person in front of us in the light of awareness, and we allow ourselves to become conscious of any pain or difficulty he or she may be experiencing. Think how wonderful it would be if this person were happy and completely free of difficulty.

On the in breath, visualize yourself drawing in this person's pain. Inhale it all like a cloud of gray or dark smoke. Freely and willingly vacuum up all that pain, as if our infinitely open heart and spacious mind is a karmic Hoover – a karma cleaner.

On the out breath, visualize yourself sending out light, radiating out to this person all your blessings, all the gifts you have: strength, positive energy, health, and well-being. Give away as much as you can. Breathe out your talent, your resources, your material possessions. Don't hold back. Send it out on a ray of light that expresses all your blessings and well-being. This will enrich one and all.

Now visualize one or two other people you know and like, joining the first person. Let yourself both acknowledge and feel the troubles these new people experience. Become aware of your sincere intention to help these people. Now, on the in breath, inhale all the pain and trouble in these people's lives. Then, on the out breath, send them your light – your blessing, all that you have.

Expand your care and concern to encompass everyone you know. On the in breath, visualize yourself removing their suffering; draw it in on a cloud of black smoke. Breathe out to them all your love, caring concern, and compassion; send it out on a ray of light. Let an awareness that the karma of the world is being purified permeate your consciousness.

Be aware of your most tender, loving heart. Let the warm feelings of open-hearted compassion expand. Visualize one or more people who have given you a difficult time – people whom you need to forgive. Think about how wonderful it would be for them if they too could be free of pain and suffering. Breathe in their hardships; send them love and care on a ray of pure light that comes from the goodness of your heart.

Let your heart expand to include the entire planet and all the people and creatures on it. Give living form to your essential intention to help others. Take upon yourself the pain and suffering of the world; fearlessly breathe it in. Breathe in the darkness and let it all dissolve into the luminous, empty, openness of your infinite heart-mind, your Buddha-nature. Breathe out your light – your healing light. Let your love help heal the world. Take on the burden. It will make you stronger. Your heart will become as wide as the world.

TONGLEN PRACTICE – PART FOUR

Now visualize all those beings radiating around you filled with the light of love that you have sent out. Visualize all that light, all that love, coming back to you. Allow the healing love to fill your heart, your entire being. Feel the joy that comes from deeply connecting with and helping others.

Rest in that image. Meditate in that light. If you like, allow yourself to make a gradual transition to a natural sky-gazing meditation, water-gazing, or simple, effortless, just-being style meditation.

When we feel the pain and suffering of the world – when we can empathize with others – we naturally develop our capacity to respond with caring and compassion. When we recognize others as not much different from ourselves, we naturally feel kinship and oneness with them. This is the awakened spiritual heart in action. It cannot help responding wherever there is need.

When we realize our interconnectedness and kinship with all, we naturally respond to them as if they were our own loved ones. Thus we actualize the Golden Rule of 'Do Unto Others . . .' naturally, almost effortlessly. This is the radiant heart, the awakened Buddhist heart of Bodhicitta – the luminous heart of Dharma.

Self and others are inseparable. If we let ourselves connect and link up in community with ever-widening circles – reaching out to link hands and hearts with those near and far – we can experience a oneness and healing that surpasses understanding; we can become more fully alive, integrated, and at peace. This is the secret of spiritual connection. Making a meaningful spiritual connection in each and every part of our lives is a real possibility. It is up to each and every one of us to actually do so.

EPILOGUE

A Prayer for the New Millennium

My prayer and New Millennium Resolution is this: to dedicate this life and all my lifetimes to the selfless service of spiritual enlightenment through working for the peace, harmony, and liberation of all beings. This is our heartfelt prayer and aspiration: That we may be the greatest we that we all, together as well as individually, can possibly be.

> *May all beings everywhere*
> *be awakened, healed, peaceful, and free;*
> *May there be peace in this world,*
> *and an end to war, poverty,*
> *violence, and oppression;*
> *and may we all together*
> *complete the spiritual journey.*
> — Lama Surya Das
> Concord, Massachusetts
> January 20, 2000

APPENDIX

The Bodhicitta Practices of an Awakened Heart

Following the Mahayana tradition founded by Atisha, over the centuries other mind-training practices became an important part of Tibetan Buddhism. One ancient and timeless mind-training practice that we studied extensively when I was in retreat with my teachers was The Thirty-seven Practices of a Bodhisattva. This is the work of Thogmé Zangpo, a Tibetan who lived in the late thirteenth and early fourteenth century. Thogmé Zangpo lived in a cave, meditating day and night on loving-kindness. Legend has it that all of the wild animals living nearby so benefited from his prayers and practice that they were able to live together in peace; even the wolf and the lamb would lovingly play together.

I personally found Thogmé's Thirty-seven Practices of a Bodhisattva indispensable when I was living with twenty-three others in a three-year cloistered retreat. These practices, which were taught to me by Dilgo Khyentse Rinpoche and Tulku Pema Wangyal, sum up the essence of Buddhist morality. Reading them, we are reminded time and time again of what is important in life. The Bodhisattva represents divine love and compassion translated into human form. These thirty-seven practices represent values and indicate the virtues that Bodhisattvas, the spiritual sons and daughters of the Buddha, all cherish.

When I look back over my copies of the text and translations that we used, I find countless little notes and quotes interspersed between each of the verses. The pages were turned so many times that the paper is yellowed and worn thin around the edges. When we studied these thirty-seven practices, we read Tibetan texts and translated them word by word. Here in this version, I've tried to translate the essence of them. Following each of these short practices, I've provided a commentary based on the notes and oral teachings. To help us use these practices today, I've also added a little spur for self-reflection or self-examination.

Think of each of these thirty-seven ancient and invaluable practices as a meditation to be reflected upon. As we read them, we think about our own lives; we think about the lessons of love and compassion we need to learn; we think about the ways that we can help others, and ourselves.

THE THIRTY-SEVEN PRACTICES
OF BODHISATTVAS

1. Since we are fortunate enough to be alive and to be blessed with human bodies and intelligence, let's take advantage of this opportunity to free ourselves and others from suffering. Listen to the teachings. Reflect on what you have heard. Meditate, meditate, meditate.

The Sons and Daughters of the Buddhas all follow this practice.

COMMENTARY: A basic theme in Buddhism is the preciousness of life – all life. As human beings, we are blessed with the opportunity to walk the path of awakening, for ourselves and others as well. The time honored way of doing this is to hear the Dharma – the spiritual teachings of truth; pay attention to what you have learned; then meditate with fervor and devotion, integrating these lessons into your daily life.

SELF-EXAMINATION: On this day, am I doing the best I can to take full advantage of the wondrous opportunities for growth and meaning that life provides?

2. In life, the strongest feelings are often generated by those we love and those who make us angry. We can become so preoccupied with these reactive feelings and our emotional concerns that we lose sight of what's right and wrong. We could instead cultivate an attitude of non-attachment to our feelings and be prepared to lessen the grip of our worldly preoccupations.

The Sons and Daughters of the Buddhas all follow this practice.

COMMENTARY: Renunciation is a part of most religious traditions. We give something up in order to gain something greater. In this instance, it is suggested that we stop letting our lives be solely guided by strong feelings and worldly preoccupations; instead, choose balance and a life based on deeper principles including an understanding of what is right and what is wrong.

SELF-EXAMINATION: Am I living according to my deepest heartfelt values and principles or am I just reacting semi-consciously to the vagaries and vacillations of the moment?

3. When we withdraw from excessive worldly stimulation and learn to put a priority on simplicity and solitude, our concentration, clarity, and wisdom increases as does our confidence in the Dharma and truth we've learned.

The Sons and Daughters of the Buddhas all follow this practice.

COMMENTARY: Our lives are often so completely filled with distracting situations that we can't focus on what's important. When we find solitude and 'simplify, simplify, simplify,' as Thoreau said, our priorities become apparent. This is one of the values of retreats. Buddhist masters would often go into solitary retreat for years. In this new century, of course, we feel blessed if we can find a weekend, a day, or even an hour to meditate and reflect on ways to simplify our lives. It's wise to make certain that we find some solitary time.

SELF-EXAMINATION: Am I consistently prioritizing what really matters?

4. **This life is transient and impermanent. All the goods we've accumulated and relationships we've enjoyed will change or come to an end. The mind is like a temporary guest in our bodily house; it will someday pass beyond. Learn to think of the larger picture beyond this one lifetime.**

The Sons and Daughters of the Buddhas all follow this practice.

COMMENTARY: The Buddha said that an awareness of death can be our greatest teacher. Tibet's great yogi, Milarepa, sang:

> *'Fearing death, I went to the mountains.*
> *Over and over again I meditated on death's unpredictable*
> *coming,*
> *And took the stronghold of the deathless unchanging nature.*
> *Now I am completely beyond all fear of dying.'*

Asia is not alone in expounding this precious universal wisdom. Here in the West, the Native American Crowfoot sang in 1890:

> *'What is life?*
> *It is the flash of a firefly in the night.*
> *It is the breath of a buffalo in wintertime.*
> *It is the little shadow which runs across the grass and loses itself*
> *In the sunset.'*
>
> *– Crowfoot, 1890*

SELF-EXAMINATION: Am I living with a consciousness of my mortality, as if each day, hour, or minute could be my last?

5. If we spend our time with those who don't understand, encourage, and value our spiritual concerns, we will lose interest in truth and Dharma. As a result, we will meditate and pray less; we will lose sight of our vow to practice love and compassion for all others. Don't surround yourself with people who don't support your spiritual aspirations.

The Sons and Daughters of the Buddhas all follow this practice.

COMMENTARY: When walking the spiritual path, it's wise to avoid people whose conduct and influence pulls us in other directions away from our goals. Someone once said that if you want to know what a person values, look at his or her friends. Khyentse Rinpoche said, 'A clear, pure crystal takes on the color of the cloth upon which it is placed, whether white, yellow, red, or black. Likewise the people you spend your time with, whether their influence is good or bad, will make a huge difference to the direction your life and internal practice take.'

SELF-EXAMINATION: Do I seek out meaningful, fulfilling relationships and connections or do I gravitate toward people who pull me away from my spiritual path?

6. Good teachers and spiritual friends help us solve our problems and maintain our loving intentions. Cherish these kindred spirits, friends, and mentors.

The Sons and Daughters of the Buddhas all follow this practice.

COMMENTARY: As seekers, we need to cultivate a community of spiritual friends who will understand and value our goals. Reach out and strengthen these connections. Appreciate and value the healing gifts that these friends provide. Seek a wise teacher.

SELF-EXAMINATION: Do I fully appreciate, respect, and attend to my spiritual mentors, friends, and teachers while they are here to help guide me?

7. **How can you expect the successful wheelers and dealers of this world to help you when they themselves are mired in worldly woes? Instead, look for refuge and support in what's real and reliable.**

The Sons and Daughters of the Buddhas all follow this practice.

COMMENTARY: In life, when we find ourselves in crisis, we sometimes look for support, love, or guidance in all the wrong places. In Buddhism it is taught that we can consistently turn for help and solace to what is tried and true – the Three Jewels: the enlightened teacher; the liberating teachings; and spiritual friends/community.

SELF-EXAMINATION: Am I looking for what I need in places where it can be found?

8. **The Buddha said that our suffering and confusion is the result of our negative actions. Understand this and turn away from all behaviors that are harmful to self and others.**

Use all your strength to resist any tendency to cause harm to anyone.

The Sons and Daughters of the Buddhas all follow this practice.

COMMENTARY: When we hurt others, we run the risk that our actions will boomerang back on ourselves. In some cases, we feel the repercussions immediately – often with our own immediate guilt, if not worse forms of instant karma. Other times, it may take years or lifetimes. But the laws of cause and effect are very clear. An essential spiritual rule: *Do no harm.* Cultivate the good. Be as good as you intrinsically are.

SELF-EXAMINATION: Am I scrutinizing all my thoughts and actions for any trace of nonbeneficial or unwholesome motivation?

9. The worldly pleasures we pursue in the course of our lives can vanish in an instant, like dew on the tip of a blade of grass. There is greater satisfaction and lasting bliss to be found in walking the spiritual path and awakening the Buddha within.

The Sons and Daughters of the Buddhas all follow this practice.

COMMENTARY: It's foolish to turn away from the path of awakening merely to fulfill our quest for pleasure. No matter how good something looks, feels, sounds, or tastes, this pleasure will last for little more than a heartbeat. Enlightenment, on the other hand, brings us freedom and bliss.

SELF-EXAMINATION: Am I too easily distracted by 'cheap thrills' or am I able to keep my eye on the bigger picture?

10. **How can we think only of ourselves when others are suffering? Recognize this suffering and generate the awakened heart-mind of Bodhicitta for the benefit of all.**

The Sons and Daughters of the Buddhas all follow this practice.

COMMENTARY: Ancient Buddhist texts point out that we have all been reborn so many times that every single living creature has at one time been a loving relative, perhaps even our mother or father. These old friends and loved ones may be suffering; they may need our help. The greatest service we can provide is to cultivate and radiate Bodhicitta – the awakened heart-mind – throughout the universe.

SELF-EXAMINATION: Am I sensitive to what others are experiencing?

11. **Selfish thoughts and desires will ultimately fail us. Replace these concerns with compassion for all others and the greater good. This will lead us to freedom and awakening.**

The Sons and Daughters of the Buddhas all follow this practice.

COMMENTARY: Self-interest is our spiritual foe. When we think only of ourselves, we cause problems for ourselves. Cultivating love and a greater awareness of others bring us closer to spiritual maturity and great awakening. Shantideva said:

> *All the joy the world contains*
> *Has come through wishing happiness for others.*
> *All the misery the world contains*
> *Has come through wanting pleasure for oneself.*

SELF-EXAMINATION: According to Buddhist wisdom, egotism and selfishness is the root of all evil. How can this teaching help me release my own self-absorption and egotism?

12. Cultivate a nonattachment for worldly goods that is so strong that even if someone takes away everything you own, you will still feel compassion and pray for his prosperity and well-being.

The Sons and Daughters of the Buddhas all follow this practice.

COMMENTARY: We can use our monetary and worldly losses to accelerate our spiritual growth. I have a little story about this. Recently I was walking down a street on a country road in Vermont, and came upon a yard sale. I stopped to look at the various dishes, bric a brac, and clothing that had been collected. The woman who was running the sale was laughing ruefully. It seems that moments before, a car had pulled up, and while her back was turned, the driver had taken several men's shirts, jackets, and slacks that were hanging on a tree. The car then sped away. 'Well,' she said, 'I hope somebody enjoys the clothes, and I hope everything fits.' That was my lesson for the day! Of course, these were just small items. But this is the kind of attitude we need to extend to everyone, even those who cause us large financial loss, if we wish to truly transcend attachment to worldly possessions and experience content and abundance.

SELF-EXAMINATION: Can I share whatever I have, recognizing that nothing is really mine for very long anyway?

13. If we should know someone who threatens us or tries to cause us serious bodily harm, we should feel compassion for this person and show mercy by genuinely wishing that he suffers no further because of his or her deluded and misguided state.

The Sons and Daughters of the Buddhas all follow this practice.

COMMENTARY: The last two practices are very similar to the words of Jesus found in the New Testament book of Matthew:

'But I say to you, Do not resist an evildoer. But if anyone strikes you on the right cheek, turn the other also; and if anyone wants to sue you and take your coat, give your cloak as well; and if anyone forces you to go one mile, go also the second mile. Give to anyone who begs from you, and do not refuse anyone who wants to borrow from you. You have heard that it was said, "You shall love your neighbor and hate your enemy." But I say to you, Love your enemies and pray for those who persecute you.'

SELF-EXAMINATION: Can I feel compassion even for

those who wish me ill? Can I remember that they are actually harming themselves?

14. **Even if someone slanders and criticizes us, spreading cruel rumors that some people may even believe, speak of that person with kindness. When you speak of him to others, praise his virtues.**

The Sons and Daughters of the Buddhas all follow this practice.

COMMENTARY: When someone says unkind things about us that aren't true, it feels very mean. No one wants to be slandered. Nonetheless, when it happens, we can pray that the person gains peace and overcomes the prejudices, misconceptions, and mental instability that must be at work. My teacher, Dilgo Khyentse Rinpoche, said, 'To reply with kindness and compassion to negativity and harm is the swiftest way to progress in overcoming ego and fulfilling the Bodhisattva path.'

SELF-EXAMINATION: Do we have the inner strength and fortitude to respond both intelligently and gently to the inevitable diversity of opinions that exist in our world?

15. **Even if someone insults and criticizes us in front of others, describing our flaws to anyone who will listen, instead of feeling anger, consider that person like a spiritual friend and advisor. Listen quietly and show respect; we can always learn from honest criticism.**

The Sons and Daughters of the Buddhas all follow this practice.

COMMENTARY: There is a distinction between this practice and the one immediately preceding it. Here, the person who is pointing out our flaws may be abusing us with harsh words, but nonetheless, the criticism has some validity. We are doubly advised against becoming defensive and angry because this person has taken on a role not unlike that of a true teacher who helps us see our shortcomings so we can work on ourselves. Dilgo Khyentse Rinpoche said, 'If someone criticizes us, why should we be unhappy? Someone else may be praising us at the same time. How does either really affect us?'

SELF-EXAMINATION: Am I open to constructive criticism and learning from even hostile opinions?

16. If someone we have nurtured and cared for as one would a cherished child becomes resentful, angry, and hurtful, we should become even kinder and more giving; we should be understanding.

The Sons and Daughters of the Buddhas all follow this practice.

COMMENTARY: Many of us have had the experience of trying to treat someone with kindness and love only to have the person turn on us for reasons we don't fully understand. Unkindness from someone we love is so much more painful than abuse from a stranger. Even so, we are encouraged to maintain our affectionate and loving attitude as if toward someone who is ill or not in his/her right mind.

SELF-EXAMINATION: Can I continue to feel love and empathy even for those who I feel have betrayed me?

17. If someone is contemptuous or treats you without respect – even if that person is not your intellectual or spiritual equal – repay them with honor as you would an admired teacher.

The Sons and Daughters of the Buddhas all follow this practice.

COMMENTARY: We train ourselves to swallow our pride; as we do so we realize that every time someone treats us with contempt and lack of respect, we are being given a lesson in humility. This lesson is all the stronger when it is delivered by someone we don't want to think of as our equal or qualified to correct us. This helps us loosen attachment to ego. With this practice, we can begin to realize that we are all equally important; we all have our opinions and a right to express them.

SELF-EXAMINATION: Do I genuinely understand the valuable lessons to be found through humility?

18. No matter how dire your emotional, physical, or financial condition, stay true to your practice, your inner principles, and your intentions. Continue to walk the path of awakening for yourself and all beings.

The Sons and Daughters of the Buddhas all follow this practice.

COMMENTARY: In Buddhism we are taught to bring everything in our lives – good and bad – onto the spiritual path. Some of the most inspiring practitioners are those whose lives are filled with serious problems, illness, and personal loss; even so, they stay committed to the Bodhisattva Vow and the spiritual path. In this way, even stumbling blocks are stepping stones.

SELF-EXAMINATION: At the most difficult moments in my life, can I stay open-hearted and maintain my commitment to the path of enlightenment?

19. **Success and fame can be detrimental to spiritual development. No matter how much wealth you accumulate or how much you are praised and admired, don't be swept away by worldly achievements or lose sight of what is real. Stay connected to who you are and what really matters.**

The Sons and Daughters of the Buddhas all follow this practice.

COMMENTARY: When we are trying to have a spiritual practice, money and success sometimes present a genuine challenge. It's easy to forget that praise and gain are merely transitory and lack any real substance. We've all seen how easy it is for successful people to get swept away on ego trips and lose touch with fundamental values. This practice reminds us to stay grounded in what's real, true, and good.

SELF-EXAMINATION: It's difficult not to get swept up into an ego trip when everything is going well. Can I do it? Can I stay committed to an awakened heart and bring my happy days with me on the spiritual path?

20. **Anger is an inner problem. When you feel anger, don't just strike out at others. Instead turn inward and call upon your resources of awareness, love, and compassion to heal yourself first.**

The Sons and Daughters of the Buddhas all follow this practice.

COMMENTARY: It's been said many times: How can we heal others unless we can heal ourselves? The powerful emotion of anger can create havoc, causing us to hurt others as well as ourselves. Think about the situations that have made you respond or even lash out with anger. We heal our anger with forgiveness – forgiveness of ourselves as well as others.

SELF-EXAMINATION: Thich Nhat Hanh reminds his students that 'anger makes us ugly . . . anger makes us suffer . . . anger makes us double up like a shrimp being roasted.' Can I remember this insight the next time I feel anger arising?

21. The more we pursue our desires, the more our desires grow; it's like drinking saltwater. We find freedom by letting go of our tendencies to become obsessed and addicted to situations that will ultimately prove unsatisfying.

The Sons and Daughters of the Buddhas all follow this practice.

COMMENTARY: In life, we could all become more balanced and even. Recognize our desires for what they are: ways of keeping us stuck, attached, and addicted. Satisfaction arises from seeking wholeness and well-being rather than seeking excitement. All else is like a roller-coaster.

SELF-EXAMINATION: Am I sometimes like a moth who is attracted to a flame? Do I become consumed by the objects of my momentary desire?

22. **Recognize that life is dreamlike and illusory, and that truth is beyond concepts, existence, or solid separate individuality. See what** *is;* **move away from a dualistic perception of reality.**

The Sons and Daughters of the Buddhas all follow this practice.

COMMENTARY: This practice introduces the concept of absolute Bodhicitta, which recognizes that everything is infinitely vast, ungraspable, and unknowable. Shabkar, a renowned, enlightened Tibetan yogi of the nineteenth century, sang:

> *'I realized that the nature of this mind,*
> *The root of samsara and nirvana,*
> *Is an ineffable luminous void*
> *With nothing to cling to.'*

SELF-EXAMINATION: Can I keep my perspective on my experience – can I watch and enjoy the sitcom or the movie of my life without being overwhelmed by the melo-dramatic moments? Can I see through myself and not take it all so seriously?

23. **Don't be fooled by appearances, style, or form. The loveliest objects can be as insubstantial and fleeting as the rainbows of summer. Let go of your impulsive, knee-jerk attractions to things that don't last.**

The Sons and Daughters of the Buddhas all follow this practice.

COMMENTARY: Why are we so strongly attracted to beautiful people and beautiful objects? Why are we overly influenced by current styles? In this modern age, entire industries revolve around beautiful images from the shiniest new cars to the most exciting new fashion models. The teachings of the Buddha remind us to look deeper into ourselves, into each other, and into the face of life itself – not just living on the surface of things, and wading in the shallows of life.

SELF-EXAMINATION: In my life, am I able to differentiate between the commercials and the main story?

24. All of us face problems and suffering. Recognize the illusory nature of all things; regard even difficulties and tragedies as fleeting and dreamlike.

The Sons and Daughters of the Buddhas all follow this practice.

COMMENTARY: This meditation on illusion and dreams is meant to be particularly helpful for seekers who struggle with crisis, tragedy, and grief. It addresses the age-old question of why bad things happen to good people. Milarepa's beloved guru Marpa was a householder who suffered the tragic death of his teenage son. When his child died, Marpa cried, 'Of course everything is an illusion, but the death of a child is like a nightmare.' Then he cried some more.

When faced with our own tragedies, we need to remember that when it's time to grieve, we grieve; this is necessary. Our dreamlike emotions are just as valid within the dream as anything else. We keep in touch with the bigger picture by remembering that even tragedies are insubstantial and illusory.

SELF-EXAMINATION: Am I able to open my tender and vulnerable heart and feel the suffering and vicissitudes of life even while recognizing its illusory nature?

25. If we truly want enlightenment, we must be prepared to give of ourselves and all that we own without any thought of personal merit or gain. Cultivate an abundant, generous heart.

The Sons and Daughters of the Buddhas all follow this practice.

COMMENTARY: This charitable practice refers to the first paramita, generosity. The Sanskrit word 'paramita' is literally translated as 'that which has reached the other shore.' In other words, a paramita refers to a transcendental virtue. The most common translation for paramita is 'perfection.' Mahayana teachings tell us to cultivate six perfections or paramitas. The first perfection that a Bodhisattva cultivates is giving with an open heart – 'open hands, open heart, open arms, and open mind.' Giving in this sense refers to more than giving alms. It means giving boundless energy and unconditional love in whatever form is required.

SELF-EXAMINATION: Can I truly be there for others, responding generously to what they need – as opposed to just giving those things that are easy for me to share?

26. If we lack ethics, virtue, and morality in our own lives, how can we help others? Practice self-discipline and moderation, vowing to be moral and ethical in everything you do.

The Sons and Daughters of the Buddhas all follow this practice.

COMMENTARY: The second paramita that a Bodhisattva cultivates is virtue and morality, which is known as 'sila.' Thus budding Bodhisattvas strive to live always with ethics, honesty, straightforwardness, and virtue. This leads to character development, self-mastery, and the spiritual refinement of an impeccable, fully actualized human being.

SELF-EXAMINATION: Do I apply ethical principles to my daily decisions whether they be large or small?

27. Our worthwhile intentions are continually challenged by the negative and destructive situations we encounter. In the most trying circumstances, let go of anger and resentment. Instead cultivate patience toward all.

The Sons and Daughters of the Buddhas all follow this practice.

COMMENTARY: The third paramita is 'shanti' – the perfection of patience, endurance, and forbearance. We can learn to 'go beyond' the expectations of this world and display patience in the most intolerable situations. During his lifetime, the Buddha's cousin tried to kill him. The Buddha said that this cousin's behavior helped him develop even greater patience, forbearance, and compassion. The Buddha referred often to this cousin as one of his best teachers.

SELF-EXAMINATION: Do I understand the importance of patience? Do I cultivate forbearance in myself in all situations?

28. Many seek to reach enlightenment for themselves alone; even they walk the path as though their hair is on fire and only their effort will put out the flames of their spiritual emergency. Think, therefore, of how much more energy is required to strive for enlightenment for the benefit of all who suffer. This goal requires total commitment, courage, and diligent effort.

The Sons and Daughters of the Buddhas all follow this practice.

COMMENTARY: The Buddha's advice to his followers was to meditate and strive for enlightenment as though their hair was on fire. This practice refers to the fourth paramita, which is the perfection of perseverance and effort. All of us innately have within us boundless energy and inexhaustible resources. We have only to utilize these inner natural resources to fulfill our heart's desire.

SELF-EXAMINATION: Do I have a passion for truth and enlightenment or am I just going through the motions?

29. In order to penetrate the nature of reality and achieve real insight and deeper understanding, we need training and grounding in mental stability and focused attention. Mere spiritual highs are not sufficient to liberate and awaken our mind, or to achieve the result of 'the heart's true release.'

The Sons and Daughters of the Buddhas all follow this practice.

COMMENTARY: This practice corresponds to the fifth paramita, the perfection of meditation, of mindfulness, focus, and concentration. If, through contemplative practices, you develop mental stability and focused concentration, then you can use it to gain deeper insight into the nature of reality. This delivers us far beyond the merely temporary highs and lows of the path of spiritual experience. These experiences are like scenery along the great highway of awakening. Better to develop insight, wisdom, and stable awareness.

SELF-EXAMINATION: Do I make the practice of self-awareness through meditation and a mindful outlook a priority in my life?

30. The perfections of generosity, virtue, patience, effort, and meditative absorption alone will not bring us to enlightenment without the cultivation of wisdom.

The Sons and Daughters of the Buddhas all follow this practice.

COMMENTARY: Wisdom, or 'prajna,' is the sixth paramita. But when we talk about wisdom, we mean perfect or transcendental wisdom, not just knowledge. This is a wisdom so complete that it is liberated from concepts. It is taught that the highest form of wisdom is insight into the true nature of reality (which is emptiness), beyond the dualism or separatist framework of subject, object, and interaction. This is the realization of 'sunyata' – infinite openness, emptiness, and oneness.

SELF-EXAMINATION: Am I accessing my inner wisdom and applying it through practical virtues? Am I understanding the emptiness of things and seeing how things work and fit together?

31. We need always continue to look inward and make consistent efforts to examine our faults in order to root out and let go of our own confusion and delusion. This requires a sincere and ongoing commitment to awakening from the sleep of illusion. Ideally we should embody the Dharma, not just pay it lip service.

The Sons and Daughters of the Buddhas all follow this practice.

COMMENTARY: It's very easy to get lax and lazy about self-examination, and even to fool ourselves. In all spiritual traditions, there are practitioners who only go so far before stalling on the side of the path, being satisfied to rest on a plateau. When he wrote this practice, Thogme Zangpo was telling us to 'walk our talk,' practice what we preach, and make it to the finish line. This is essential advice to the Dharma practitioner. Otherwise we may find ourselves becoming hypocrites who say one thing and do another.

SELF-EXAMINATION: Am I consistently practicing self-examination? Do I see myself realistically?

32. Don't speak ill of others, and don't criticize fellow seekers. The only faults we should mention are our own.

The Sons and the Daughters of the Buddhas all follow this practice.

COMMENTARY: This is simple and straightforward advice that discourages negative and judgmental criticism. Jesus' New Testament advice to his followers was, 'Why do you see the speck in your neighbor's eye, but do not notice the log in your own eye?' The Buddha told his followers to refrain from gossiping and fault-finding. He told them to use words to help, not harm others. A Tibetan saying: 'Don't look for the flea in others' hair and overlook the yak sitting on your own nose.'

SELF-EXAMINATION: Am I resisting the temptation to judge and talk about others?

33. **Sometimes our most intense emotions and arguments occur with family and good friends – those with whom we are most intimate. It can be difficult to study and reflect on the Dharma or meditate when all of our energy is engaged in domestic disputes. Avoid the strong attachments and emotions that these situations encourage.**

The Sons and Daughters of the Buddhas all follow this practice.

COMMENTARY: When it was written several hundred years ago, this practical teaching specifically addressed the daily travails of household life. At that time, there was a different class and social structure. Tibetan society was divided into the royalty, the monastic community, and the lay householders who were often patrons. When a monk became embroiled in the domestic life of a patron, valuable time was spent. Dharma teachers were well aware then of how much energy gets absorbed in the melodramas of day-to-day life. The same thing, of course, is true today, but we also realize that we can't always walk away from family, friends, colleagues, homes, and responsibilities. Nonetheless, we should be able to employ mindfulness and spiritual intentions to become less attached and invested in the roller-coaster of daily life. Instead here and now in this century, we could utilize homes and workplaces too as opportunities for spiritual growth.

SELF-EXAMINATION: Am I doing all I can to find ways to integrate my spiritual philosophy into my relationships with my close circle of friends and family?

34. Unkind words can cause great harm. When we are angry and speak harshly to others, we lose our spiritual footing. We create pain, causing someone else's mind to become disturbed and upset. Give up abusing others with harsh language.

The Sons and Daughters of the Buddhas all follow this practice.

COMMENTARY: The Buddha was very sensitive to the amount of damage and abuse that can be caused through our speech. In this practice, we are reminded that someone who has the intention of helping another must remember to speak kindly and gently.

SELF-EXAMINATION: Are my communications – my words, the tone of my voice, and my body language – healing, harmonizing, and sensitive?

35. It's all too easy to fall into unconscious ways of acting and thinking. Mindfulness helps us more closely observe ourselves and thus keep our tendencies to form negative habits in check.

The Sons and Daughters of the Buddhas all follow this practice.

COMMENTARY: Pay attention; it pays off. This is probably the shortest yet most effective advice anyone can give on how to live an enlightened life. Otherwise, we find ourselves constantly trying to play catch-up, trying to undo mistakes and errors that we have made through a lack of mindfulness. For some mistakes there are no remedies. That's why it's wisest to stay awake and conscious of what you do, say, and think.

SELF-EXAMINATION: Today, am I living mindfully – consciously, and intentionally upholding my intention to live the spiritual life?

36. In summation: **Whatever we do, whatever we think, wherever we go, whatever the circumstances, we need to look inward to examine our minds. The work of a Bodhisattva requires mindful, attentive awareness.**

The Sons and the Daughters of the Buddhas all follow this practice.

COMMENTARY: Each time we renew our Bodhisattva Vow, we are reminded that this path isn't always an easy stroll. The Bodhisattva's way of life calls for a full-time commitment to being more consciously loving and aware.

SELF-EXAMINATION: Am I remaining steadfast in my aspiration to a higher, more meaningful, and deeper life?

37. **Dedicate our practice for the good of all. Share the benefits with everyone. Include all in your heart and prayers. Recognize the interconnectedness of all and make no distinction between beings; we are all equal in the spirit.**

The Sons and Daughters of the Buddhas all follow this practice.

COMMENTARY: This final practice reaffirms the merits and good fortune to be found in practicing both relative and absolute Bodhicitta, without taking ourselves too seriously. This path is a joyous highway of awakening.

Within the Avatamsaka (Garland) Sutra, a Bodhisattva speaks several wonderful lines of poetry that get to the essence of Bodhicitta and the meaning of wisdom and nonduality.

> *'Be free from subject and object,*
> *Get away from dirtiness and cleanness,*
> *Sometimes entangled and sometimes not.*
> *I forget all relative knowledge; my real*
> *wish is to enjoy all things with all people.'*

SELF-EXAMINATION: Am I including the welfare of all beings in my heart's prayers, my spiritual practice, and my life work?

This, I think, is Buddha's love.

ABOUT THE DZOGCHEN FOUNDATION

More information about Lama Surya Das and his schedule of lectures, workshops, retreats, tapes, CDs local meditation groups, and Dzogchen training can be found at:

www.surya.org

Those without Internet access, please write or call:

The Dzogchen Foundation
P.O. Box 400734
Cambridge, MA 02140
(617) 628–1702

To order a CD of companion chants called *Chants to Awaken the Buddhist Heart*, by Lama Surya Das and Steven Halpern, contact the Dzogchen Center at the above address or at www.dzogchen.org.

DZOGCHEN
FOUNDATION

INDEX

A SELECTION OF NON-FICTION TITLES
PUBLISHED BY TRANSWORLD

THE PRICES SHOWN BELOW WERE CORRECT AT THE TIME OF GOING TO PRESS.
HOWEVER TRANSWORLD PUBLISHERS RESERVE THE RIGHT TO SHOW NEW RETAIL
PRICES ON COVERS WHICH MAY DIFFER FROM THOSE PREVIOUSLY ADVERTISED IN THE
TEXT OR ELSEWHERE.

All Transworld titles are available by post from:

Bookpost, PO Box 29, Douglas, Isle of Man, IM99 1BQ

Credit cards accepted. Please telephone 01624 836000,
fax 01624 837033, Internet http://www.bookpost.co.uk
or e-mail: bookshop@enterprise.net for details

Free postage and packing in the UK. Overseas customers:
allow £1 per book (paperbacks) and £3 per book (hardbacks)